TALKING ZEN

TALKING ZEN

Reflections on Mind, Myth, and the Magic of Life

ALAN WATTS

Edited by MARK WATTS

SHAMBHALA

Shambhala Publications, Inc.
2129 13th Street
Boulder, Colorado 80302
www.shambhala.com

Cover art: Philippe Imbert / Pechane Sumie
Cover design: Katrina Noble
Interior design: Howie Severson

9 8 7 6 5 4 3 2

Printed in the United States of America

Shambhala Publications makes every effort to print
on acid-free, recycled paper.
Shambhala Publications is distributed worldwide by
Penguin Random House, Inc., and its subsidiaries.

LIBRARY OF CONGRESS CATALOGING-IN-PUBLICATION DATA

Names: Watts, Alan, 1915–1973, author. | Watts, Mark, editor.
Title: Talking Zen: reflections on mind, myth, and the magic of life /
Alan Watts; edited by Mark Watts.
Description: Boulder: Shambhala, 2022.
Identifiers: LCCN 2021049684 | ISBN 9781645470960 (trade paperback)
Subjects: LCSH: Zen Buddhism—Essence, genius, nature.
Classification: LCC BQ9265.9 .W358 2022 |
DDC 294.3/927—dc23/eng/20220105
LC record available at https://lccn.loc.gov/2021049684

Contents

Introduction

In 1937, the twenty-one-year old Alan Watts wrote in an article entitled "What Is Zen?":

> The word *zen* is the Japanese equivalent of the Chinese ch'an, which is evolved from the Sanskrit *dhyana*—usually translated as "meditation." But it does not mean "meditation" as the word is usually translated in the West. It is less a contemplative exercise undertaken in solitude than a constant attitude of mind. It places no reliance on scriptural authority, on rites and ceremonies, and it had no dogmas or orthodox body of doctrines. Strictly speaking it has no teachings as we understand them; it is a practice rather than a theory. Creeds and doctrines are ideas about truth, and not truth itself, and the aim of Zen is to sweep away all formulae, symbols and doctrinal substitutes which stand between the individual and enlightenment.
>
> Therefore its methods are, to Westerners, somewhat alarming and seemingly irreverent. It makes fun of

logic; it turns metaphysics and theology upside down to make them look absurd. Its technique is to jolt and shock people out of their intellectual ruts into the highway of spiritual freedom. Thus a religious question will often be answered with the most commonplace observation as to the state of the weather, or even with rough treatment such as a slap on the face or an extraordinary statement which appears to mean nothing. . . . For Zen is a religion of life, not a religion about life.

"What Is Zen?" was written just a year after publication of *The Spirit of Zen* in 1936. *The Spirit of Zen* was the first of two books on Zen Buddhism by Watts. His second, *The Way of Zen,* played a key role in introducing millions of Western readers to Eastern thought in general, and to Zen in particular. Prior to 1940 Watts had also begun to speak publicly, at gatherings of the Buddhist Lodge in London and before other religious study groups in Britain. His first lectures, some of which appear in the early chapters of this work, were prepared well in advance, and in their written form exhibit a style distinguishable from his written works of the period. By 1950, however, Watts had become more comfortable as a speaker, and he rarely used more than a few general notes of subject areas to be covered. By 1960 he had mastered the ability to speak extemporaneously for hours on end, often weaving together the ideas of cultures separated by thousands of miles and many centuries. By the time of his passing in 1973 Watts had authored more than twenty significant books on comparative philosophy and recorded hundreds of hours of public lectures and seminar sessions. Today many of his books remain in print and his lectures are heard on public radio across the country on "The Love of Wisdom" series.

The following chapters present a synthesis of Alan Watts' further explorations of Zen that have been adapted from spoken word archival recordings. This is not primarily an account of how Zen evolved but is instead a story of Zen in life, of insights, tales, and experiences as they were told by the author to live audiences over a period of nearly forty years. In selecting the lectures to be included I chose the talks that embodied the spontaneous and uncontrolled aspect of Zen most fully, and which left me with a compelling feeling that something extraordinary had happened. My thanks to my associate editor Dan Johnson and to Jeffrey Hunter at Weatherhill for their assistance in the challenging endeavor of translating moving performances into written pages.

"Picture Without a Frame" is the earliest known Alan Watts lecture text, probably delivered before the Buddhist Lodge in London, circa 1933.

"The Psychology of Acceptance" was delivered in 1939 before the Analytical Psychology Club in New York.

"Mythological Motifs in Modern Science" is another lecture text, probably from the early 1940s.

"Time and Convention: Five Broadcasts" were originally broadcast over KPFA in Berkeley, California. This collection of original lecture texts, from broadcasts made in late 1954 and early 1955, was privately published in 1955.

"Biting an Iron Bull" is the first session from a seminar entitled "Inevitable Ecstasy," given aboard the S.S. *Vallejo* moored in Sausalito, California, in 1971.

"Taoist Ways" was the first session from the "Taoism" seminar at Esalen in Big Sur, California, recorded in June 1965.

"Swimming Headless" is the text of the second session at the same seminar.

"Zen Tales" is a lecture from the Japan Seminar, given to a small group on tour in Japan in the autumn of 1965.

"Zen Bones" was a "zenefit" lecture given on March 9, 1967, at the Avalon Ballroom in San Francisco to raise funds for the purchase of the Tassajara Zen Center.

—Mark Watts

Picture Without a Frame

The mind of man makes sense out of life by looking at it through frames. Within limits, something can be achieved: right and wrong can be laid down; success and failure can be determined; important and unimportant can be distinguished. By constructing a frame whose boundaries are birth and death, we can, within those limits, live out a life that appears to be meaningful and to accomplish something in terms of time. But a strange disquiet arises when we look outside the frame, for before birth we are not, and after death we leave only brief memorials. Frames are the very substance of rational knowledge, for we handle our experience of the world by putting it into classes. What "is" is defined by the frame that distinguishes it from what is not, and vice versa. Motion is defined by the frame that separates it from stillness, so that if the frame be removed and we find ourselves in a world where all is in motion, the idea of motion ceases to mean anything. This is why the logicians say that there cannot be a class of all classes, a frame including all frames—for a frame with nothing at all outside its edges would not be a frame. It would be as inconceivable as the color of the eyeball's lens.

Within human society we bring order into being and make communication possible by means of frames. We identify ourselves in terms of narrowing frames of reference—as that I am human, male, Caucasian, adult, American, professor, and so forth. When the frames are larger than human—mammal, organic, existent—they begin to lose meaning. The same is true when they become smaller than the frame designated by my proper name—tissue, cells, molecules, atoms, electrons, et cetera. Yet, large or small, every one of these identifying terms is the name of a frame, and there seems to be no way of saying or thinking what I am except in terms of frames. This gives me a peculiarly empty feeling, so that I begin to feel like the Irishman's definition of a net—"a lot of holes tied together with string."

The curious human mind has always wanted to know "what" is inside the frames, and for an answer it gets only the names of still smaller frames. In modern philosophy it is no longer considered proper to ask what anything is, unless you are simply speaking about its class or frame, or unless you are asking what it does—unless, that is, you are asking for an "operational definition." But even operational definitions—running, jumping, hopping, wobbling—are the names of frames, of classes of movement and behavior. The problem is that thought and language have no terms except frame-terms, and there is really no way of even phrasing one's question so as to speak of what is not a frame. To ask, "What?" is to ask, "What frame?" for there are no means of saying what anything is save by denoting its class, by describing its "difference" from other things, which is simply to designate its boundaries, its frame.

In many schools of philosophy, stray thoughts that quarrel with this conclusion are simply outlawed as meaningless nonsense. The philosophers must at all costs convince themselves that life is composed of frames and frames alone, overlooking the fact that frames are "airy nothings" in their enthusiasm for the fact that, hollow as they may be, they are at least definite. The philosophers will also contend that such knowledge amounts to far more than a vain effort to catch the wind in nets. After all it is the very nature of scientific knowledge; and look what science has achieved in the realm of concrete experience—at the innumerable ways in which it has made it easier and more pleasant to survive in this world as human beings.

One may wonder how close Western philosophy is coming to a realization that the "real material world" composed entirely of these frames is a vast net of abstractions. This will, perhaps, be difficult to see so long as we pretend to be really satisfied with the technological miracles of science—so long as the prospects of longer and more pleasant lives can distract our attention and keep it well within the limits of the frame called birth-and-death. But people have never been willing to remain closed in boxes for very long, and the wiser orthodoxies have used them as wise parents provide playpens for their babies. On the one hand, the pen is a safe place where baby can stay out of trouble. On the other, there is a proper parental pride in seeing the baby grow strong enough to climb over the fence. The trouble with so many Western orthodoxies is that they have been living inside the pen with the baby. They have never allowed those who went outside to return unless they promise never to go out again. It is for this reason that the great Western orthodoxies, religious and scientific, have been strictly exoteric and profane. They have never had the secret smile of the parent who lays down rules in the hope that they will eventually be disobeyed. But that is the smile on the face of the sphinx, and on the faces of meditating buddhas.

To know the universe in terms of nothing but frames is almost exactly what Indian philosophy means by *maya*, the idea that all such knowledge is in some sense an illusion. The very word is related to our terms *metre, matrix,* and *material* since it comes from the Sanskirt root *ma,* "to measure." And measurement is framing: describing, as circles are described with dividers; defining, as limits are set with rulers; and dividing with hairlines, as minutes are marked out on a clock. These make up the frail mesh of abstractions with which the human mind tries to grasp the world, always, ultimately, in vain. For the sense of achievement, whether in knowledge or in action, is maintained only so long as one keeps one's gaze within a limited frame. But if the angle of vision is widened in both space and time, we begin to feel a frightening sense of futility. It begins to dawn upon us that our knowledge of the world and of ourselves is entirely hollow, and that all our efforts of muscle and brain have gone for nothing.

A despair of this kind is the starting point of Buddhism. But those who close their minds to it never discover that despair has two faces—that the sigh of "giving up the ghost" transforms itself into the sigh of relief, of liberation. This is, I think, the proper meaning of *nirvana* "to blow out, to despirate." It is here, too, that we discover the meaning of Buddhist and Taoist passivity, of the peculiar wisdom of a certain almost indescribable kind of inaction.

If there is any one psychological problem that really baffles the student of Buddhism, it is that desire (*trishna*) or grasping cannot put an end to desire—or, in other words, that to seek awakening (*bodhi*) is to thrust it away, that to try to become a buddha is to perpetuate ignorance. To imagine that the self can deliver itself is to foster the very illusion of self that constitutes bondage. For when awakening, the actual vision of reality, is conceived as something to be grasped, something to be reached in the course of future time as if it were an object of success, then it is at once degraded to the level of frame-knowledge. Hence the strange insistence of such Zen masters as Rinzai and Bankei on the life of "not seeking."

In the words of Rinzai, "Don't have a single thought in your mind about seeking for buddhahood." How can this be? The ancients say, "If you desire deliberately to seek the buddha, your buddha is just *samsara* (birth and death)." There is no place in Buddhism for using effort. Just be ordinary, without anything special. Relieve your bowels, pass water, put on your clothes, and eat your food. When you're tired, go and lie down. Ignorant people may laugh at me, but the wise will understand. If a man seeks the Tao, that man loses the Tao.[1]

Or, as Suzuki translates the words of Bankei, "If you have the least desire to be something better than you actually are, if you hurry up to the slightest degree in your search of something, you are already going against the unborn [i.e., the unframed]."[2]

It is at this point that the *jiriki* ("self-powered") and *tariki* ("other-powered") forms of Buddhism meet, for Rinzai and Bankei are here saying what the followers of the Jodo Shinshu, or True Pure Land School, express in other terms. According to their view, the notion that a person can attain buddhahood by their own effort or contriving is sheer pride. One must recognize that one's own resources can lead nowhere but to the *naraka,* the so-called hells, the places of perpetual self-frustration. Deliverance from this bondage must come through a complete disillusionment with one's own efforts, in which there is no recourse but to trust oneself completely to the "other-power." This requires the total abandonment of all forms of "self-powered" thinking, including the concern as to whether one's faith is sufficient or sincere.[3]

The difficulty of realizing this total abandonment of seeking or "self-power" is that the notion "I must do something to get it" is so deeply ingrained that even giving up or "not doing" is approached in the spirit of something to be done. This is why the Pure Land School insists that even concern as to whether one has faith or the power of self-surrender is to be abandoned, and why Zen says: "This cannot be attained through thinking; this cannot be sought by not thinking."

This is to say the same thing as when Suzuki quotes from the Pure Land mystic Kichibei, "When all the ideas of self-power based upon moral values and disciplinary measures are purged, there is nothing left in you that will declare itself to be the hearer [i.e., the one who gives up and accepts the other-power], and just because of this you do not miss anything you hear."[4]

Self-surrender is not, then, a voluntary act, but something that happens when one finds themself in an ultimate quandary, at a crossroads where every road offered is the wrong road, and every choice, even making no choice, is a mistake. The function of such Buddhist disciplines as meditation and the *koan* is to precipitate this quandary, to exhibit the futility of "self-power" by exercising it to the limit. Yet such meditations become somewhat farcical when done in order to realize what cannot be done, when, as it were, you try to make a catch hold of itself "in order" to realize that it can't. Of such artificial efforts to get oneself into this quandary, which Zen calls the state of "great doubt," Bankei said, "It is like a Buddhist priest misplacing his only ceremonial robe, which he fails to locate in spite of his most anxious hunting. He or she cannot even for a moment give up the thought of the lost article. This is a doubt genuinely aroused. People of these days try to cherish doubt merely because the old masters had it. This no more than make-believe: it is like searching after a thing that one has never lost."[5]

Our difficulty in understanding such men as Rinzai, Bankei, and Kichibei is that their Buddhism sounds too easy. To judge from their words, the great buddhas and sages realized a state of mind so close to our ordinary everyday mind that we seem forced to one of two conclusions: that there is nothing specially important in Buddhism after all, or that we have completely misunderstood what they were saying. It seems inconceivable that these spiritual giants of the past should have gone through all their disciplines and labors for nothing, so that in the end all that they have to say is, as Nansen said to Joshu, "Your ordinary mind is the Tao, and by intending to accord with it, you immediately deviate."

But the problem here is, again, one of framework. Buddhism was originally no more than the Buddha's experience of awakening. After twenty-five hundred years of explanation and discussion it has been so conformed to the frames of human thought that our view of what a buddha is has undergone a radical distortion. Our very natural reverence for these spiritual giants, coupled with the intensity of our aspiration to the same state, has inevitably made awakening a coveted prize. It has, in other words, raised it to the very highest degree of a scale of values in which it has no part at all: the scale of success. Yet it would be nearer to the point, though still short of it, to say that awakening is ultimate failure.

In the symbolism of the Buddhist Wheel of Becoming, the state of buddhahood lies nowhere in the six divisions of the Wheel. At the highest point are the *devas,* the angels at the very crown of spiritual success. But, on the circular path, high leads to low, and in the depths are the *naraka* realms that represent the extreme of sentient misery. Ascent does not lead to *nirvana*, to buddhahood, but only to the temporary *deva* world. In other words, there can be no association of awakening with ideas of attainment, of spiritual superiority, of success, of mastery, or of claims to any prerogative. It is only quite figuratively—that is, within the misleading frames of human thought—that the buddhas are termed higher than Ishvara, higher than the highest gods. "Higher" must here be translated as meaning "altogether outside the scale of values in which high and low have any significance."

Yet, on the other hand, the state of awakening is just as remote from that envious hostility to greatness, that insensitive disregard for the relative values of superiority that expresses itself in shallow egalitarianism. This is a kind of profane mimicry of the classlessness of the buddhas, which is by no means freedom from class, but mere antagonism to it. And antagonism is another form of bondage.

The status of a buddha is immeasurable, not because of its height or depth, but because buddhas do not measure, so are not *maya,* and so, in a way, do not matter. It is all the same word. They are, in Zen language, *buji* ("nothing special") without affecting to be ordinary. Above all, to a buddha it is meaningless to think that he or she is a buddha. For there is no "he or she," no frame.

The Psychology of Acceptance

The Reconciliation of the Opposites in
Eastern Thought and in Analytical Psychology

Before I begin this lecture, I must warn you that I am going to discuss the most irritating and elusive subject in the world. The subject itself concerns perhaps the most important problem of humankind's spiritual life, and I said that it was irritating and elusive because it is so essentially simple that the moment we begin to grapple with it, it becomes unutterably complicated. I am afraid I have been guilty of a paradox, but it is said that a paradox is only a truth standing on its head to attract attention. There are certain truths that have to be stood on their heads before they can be noticed at all; in the ordinary way they are so simple that we fail to perceive them, and they have to be complicated in order to be presented for thought and discussion. Our own faces are an example of this. Nothing could be more obvious and self-evident than a person's own face; but oddly enough, the person cannot see it at all unless they introduce the complication of a mirror that shows it to them reversed. The image one sees is their face and yet not their face, and this is a form of paradox. If this is true of a person's face, how much more must it be true of their innermost self, their soul, psyche, mind, or whatever you like to call it? If the eyes cannot see themselves, how much less can that something which looks through the eyes see itself? And yet this something is, generally speaking, the most important and the most predominant factor in our lives; it hardly ever passes out of direct or indirect consciousness, and yet the moment we try to lay hold on it, we find ourselves in a maze of confusion. So peculiar is this thing that we call the "self" or "soul" that when something goes wrong with it, it finds it so hard to put it right that it must resort to the astonishing procedure of visiting a psychologist—who is a kind of mental mirror—and with them submit to a devastatingly complex analysis that may last months or years.

Therefore, complications inevitably arise whenever we approach the affairs of the spirit. To use another illustration, nothing could be more simple and ordinary than water. But try to grasp it in your hands, and you will go on grasping to your dying day, for the harder you grasp, the faster it slips through your fingers. Two definitions are called for at this point. What is this thing that I have called the self, soul, or psyche, and what is meant by a person's spirit or spiritual life? With regard to the self, we will enter into no more complications than are absolutely necessary. For the time being, call it just the thing that feels that it is "I," that which perceives and knows, which appears to be able to exist in both conscious and unconscious states. You refer to it subjectively as I, and objectively as myself. But, as to "spirit" and "spiritual" I am wondering whether I ought to use such words at all in a scientific assembly. Perhaps, though, you will pardon their use if I explain that I mean by them nothing occult, supernatural, metaphysical, or psychic; nothing, in fact, that is outside the scope of our ordinary, everyday consciousness. To my mind, the affairs of the spirit concern a certain type of relationship between the self and the universe, the external universe of people, things, institutions, natural forces, and the like, and the internal universe of ideas, feelings, and impulses both conscious and unconscious. But what type of relationship is this? In one sense, it is a psychological adjustment to these inner and outer worlds. In this sense spirituality is entirely a matter of adjustment, and has nothing to do with supernatural or psychic perceptions or entities, nor with anything that we may understand as an occult state of consciousness.

Thus, we may say that there is spiritual growth when a person becomes so adjusted to the world that he or she is at ease and at home with both conscious perceptions and unconscious impulses. That is using psychological terminology, but if we were to put it into the language of religion, we should say that a person in this condition loved and was at one with life in all its aspects. Psychology and religion alike exist because, as a general rule, people lack this adjustment. They are oppressed by external circumstances and the uncontrolled whims of their own mind; they are involved between conflicting pairs of opposites—pleasure and pain, life and death, love and fear, good and evil—and their maladjustment consists, apparently, in holding to one of these opposites and rejecting the other. There is the primary opposition between oneself and all that is not oneself, between the subjective and objective worlds, and one resists and tries to escape from all those things in the objective world that cause one pain or threaten their existence, and here the complications begin. I am not going to inquire into the original cause of this condition of suffering, this resistance to life that seems to increase as humankind ascends from the primitive state; for the purpose of this discussion we must just take it as existing, and leave other questions to academic theologians.

Therefore, we must begin with the premise that in one way or another we suffer from this opposition between ourselves and the world. Disliking this state of affairs, we create an ideal called happiness, which may mean one of two things: either the elimination of all those things about us that cause pain or else a state of mind of psychological adaptation, whereby we can accept pain and so conquer it. That is not to say that this acceptance removes pain-causing events; it is intended rather to remove our fear of them. Religions have come into being to create both these kinds of happiness, and religion in its most elementary form is an affair of magic designed to remove pain-causing events. This is also the purpose of physical science, and, as a rule, when one fails to achieve this purpose, they resort to some emotional, sensual, or intellectual stimulus that enables them to forget these events in the manner of the ostrich, who tries to avoid their enemy by burying their own head so that they cannot see them. But there are forms of religion, and now forms of science, that seek neither to remove painful events nor to hide from them. These forms of religion are mainly Asian in origin, and in science we find a similar purpose. The important forms of Eastern religion have a like purpose, but there you will not find any formulated concept of the unconscious as we understand it. The reason is that ancient practitioners of yoga in all its many forms were conscious of these mental contents that are unconscious to us. Thus, you will find in many yoga texts that one of the first exercises in meditation is to relax the mind in such a way that all its contents gradually rise to the surface; the texts go on to say that you will find yourself thinking of all kinds of terrible things, things that you never dreamed could exist in your soul.

But now let us go back and consider humankind in this state of opposition and consequent suffering. In their attempts to extricate themselves from it, people become involved in a terrible complexity. They fear pain, death, deprivation, and all forms of disease. Desiring to escape from these things, they fear them all the more; desiring to escape from this fear, they become afraid of fear, and then afraid of the fear of fear until they find themselves running away into an infinite regression, so that they become progressively removed from basic facts. This business of infinite regression is really the key to my whole argument, for this is in fact the fundamental program of psychology and religion alike, the thing that involves the simplicity of humankind's spiritual life in such wild complications. Infinite regression is primarily the process of a person trying to discover themself and change and know themself. It is as if they were trying to lift themself up by their own belt, as if they were spinning 'round in circles to try and see their own eyes, and the faster they spin, the faster their eyes run away. It is rather like the old story of the donkey who has a carrot dangled before them from a stick that is fastened to their collar; the more they chase it, the more it runs away, and this is infinite regression.

From this point, I want to try and describe a process of psychological development, taking analytical psychology and certain forms of Eastern religion hand in hand as far as they will go. I say "as far as they will go" because I believe there is something new that the East can contribute to this process, something so essentially simple that it is generally overlooked, something that you may think me quite crazy for introducing at all. It is a principle that one either understands or ridicules, that is seen either as a tremendous truth or else as something that is as incomprehensible as it is absurd. In the words of the Chinese sage Lao-tzu:

> When the superior man hears of the Tao,
> He puts it into practice.
> But when the inferior man hears of it, he laughs at it.
> Indeed, it would not be the true Tao if he did not laugh.
> So please do not say that you have not been warned!

But first we must lead up to this by considering the whole matter of acceptance as a principle of psychological healing. Since the birth of psychology, we have heard much about the ill effects of escaping from life—a phrase that may mean almost anything in accordance with what you understand by life, and it can be quite plausibly argued that almost any form of human activity is such an escape. Thus, for purposes of discussion, we must temporarily limit its meaning to the general reaction of human beings to any form of mental or physical suffering. We shall have to limit its meaning just a bit more than this, because there is no need to place medicine and other methods of alleviating suffering under the category of escapism. Furthermore, this is no question of moralizing and saying, "My good people, go out and suffer as much as you can. It will do you such a lot of good." Escapism, in this sense, is not avoiding suffering; it is, rather, the fear of suffering, the refusal to accept the dark side of life whenever it happens to appear. This statement will later have to be qualified, though for the time being it must stand as a starting point for our argument. The technique of acceptance is used in psychology to overcome the wish to escape and its resultant complications or neuroses. It is relaxation of a certain mental tension, which, on the one hand, represses the various unwelcome contents of the unconscious, and, on the other, reacts with fear against adversity from outside. But, it may be asked, why do scientists worry about removing fear when it might well be possible for them to remove the causes of fear through medicine, scientific economics, mechanical invention, and compulsory surgical operations on the brains of criminals and other persons with socially subversive ideas? The answer is surely that they would create an exceedingly dull world, for if there is to be a light side to life at all, there must also be a dark side. An excess of light makes the eyes blind, for too much of a good thing invariably ends in boredom, in a deadening of the senses, in a loss of the power to appreciate, and this is the first and most obvious argument in favor of acceptance. Pain is essential to pleasure if pleasure is to be known as such, for the two are to each other as back to front and short to long. Therefore, it is absurd to cling to the one and try to push the other out of existence. The same may be said of living and dying, for life is such that it depends absolutely on death, being a ceaseless process of living and dying, beginning and ending, starting and stopping, ascending and descending. Without these things, there could be no movement, no growth, nothing at all that we could call life. For just as music depends on the sounding and silencing of notes, existence depends on living and dying, the two opposites that are its father and mother. Thus, to deny and attempt to reject any one of these opposites amounts to a denial of existence itself; if, however, both are accepted, then we may say that whoever does so is at ease and at home in the world, that they have, so to speak, identified themself with the child of the opposites that is life in all its aspects. This is the philosophical justification of acceptance.

But now what about psychology? Here acceptance has a twofold function. On the one hand, the tension in the psyche that we call "escapism" must be relaxed in order that the repressed contents of the unconscious may be brought to light; on the other, the relaxation must be maintained in order that we may come to terms with those contents, having exposed them, and also that we may improve the relations between ourselves and external circumstances. The first of these functions Jung describes very admirably in his commentary to *The Secret of the Golden Flower:*

> We must be able to let things happen in the psyche. . . . Consciousness is forever interfering, helping, correcting and negating, and never leaving the simple growth of the psychic processes in peace. . . . He goes on to say that acceptance . . . consists solely in watching objectively the development of any fragment of fantasy. . . . These exercises must be continued until the cramp in the conscious is released, or, in other words, until one can let things happen; which was the immediate goal of the exercise. In this way, a new attitude is created, an attitude which accepts the irrational and the unbelievable, simply because it is what is happening.

Note that last sentence. Here is our link with the Asian view of acceptance, for Jung implies that whatever IS is to be accepted, however irrational, however ugly and unpalatable. The Hindu would say the same thing in another way, using religious terminology, for his or her philosophy of Advaita Vedanta teaches that all things are *brahman,* the breath of life, the one reality that is the *raison d'etre* of existence. Nothing, however vile and unpleasant, is anything but *brahman,* and this is another way of saying that every conceivable aspect of life is acceptable because it is an essential component of the whole. What is the psychological effect of this attitude? To answer this, let us turn to the Chinese doctrine of Taoism, which is a kind of spiritual *jujutsu* whose central principle is called "non-action," which is to say "relaxing oneself to adversity and thereby defeating it." Chuang Tzu, one of its chief exponents, says: "The perfect man employs his mind as a mirror; it grasps nothing; it refuses nothing; it receives, but does not keep." Or to use another favorite Taoist analogy, the mind is made like water, yielding to everything that may be thrust into it. And because it always yields, it can never be harmed; you may slash it forever with a knife without leaving any cut, and yet it never resists you.

An even more definite expression of the principle of acceptance will be found in the following dialogue of a Chinese teacher of Ch'an Buddhism, better known by its Japanese name Zen, and his pupil. The pupil asked him, "It is terribly hot, and how shall we escape the heat?" Instantly the teacher replied, "Go right down to the bottom of the furnace!" "But in the furnace," cried the bewildered pupil, "how shall we escape the scorching fire?" To this he gave the laconic answer, "No further pains will harass you." To one who is in the midst of mental or physical pain, this may sound like a rather bold experiment. But however absurd it sounds, in such an extremity anything is worth trying. "Go right down to the bottom of the furnace." In other words, experience pain to the full.

Do not try to run away from it, do not resist it by trying to think of something else or by cursing fate. Open your arms to it, embrace it, ask it to do its worst to you; it is a kind of "higher masochism." Everyone knows that if you do not want a nettle to sting you, you must grasp it firmly in your hand. For to run away from pain is to create a state of conflict that only inflames the hurt; it seems the obvious thing to do, just as the first instinct of a person swept away by the current is to fight against it. To go with it requires a moment's plucking up of courage; it seems to invite disaster, yet oddly enough it is the only salvation. For the attempt to escape from pain is the beginning of infinite regression, the entrance to a hideous abyss of suffering into which it is peculiarly easy to fall. In escaping, you are putting one tension on top of another, adding frost over snow, trying to quench fire with flame.

You will all be familiar with the application of this technique in analytical psychology, with Jung's idea of letting the unconscious in the form of *anima* or *animus* speak to you, of becoming acquainted with the strange emotions and impulses that take hold of you and refuse to be hurried away, inviting them, as it were, to come and have a drink and talk things over. When you no longer resist them, they no longer master you, for their power over you is derived solely from the force you pit against them. Being part of you, they simply use your strength, but if you make no show of strength, they make none either. Eventually you become master in your own house, but oh, be careful! There is a great snag coming. If you turn to Jung's *Two Essays on Analytical Psychology,* you will find in Part II one of the most important chapters he has ever written, entitled "The Mana Personality." Here he explains that having mastered the *animus* or *anima,* by acceptance you have captured for yourself what primitive peoples would call its *mana* or magic power over you. But there is a danger that this *mana* may inflate you and make you imagine yourself as a *"mana* personality," which is to say, a person of might, a magician, or god. He writes:

> If the ego arrogates to itself power over the unconscious, the unconscious responds with a subtle attack, in this case with the *mana* personality dominant, the enormous prestige of which casts a spell over the ego. The only protection against this is the fullest confession of one's own weakness over against the powers of the unconscious. We set up no power in opposition to the unconscious, and consequently we do not provoke it to attack.

But the snag is not ended here; indeed, we are only just beginning to get into trouble.

In this affair of the *mana* personality, Jung has demonstrated an important form of the difficulty that so easily turns the psychology of acceptance into an infallible method for producing lunatics. For the spell of the *mana* personality can only capture those whose acceptance has not been genuine; nothing, however, is more elusive than genuine acceptance of life. This is easy to understand when we ask why it

should ever occur to anyone in the first place that it is necessary to accept life. Let us take, for example, a person who
contracts some form of neurosis by trying to escape from pain
and the fear of pain. They go to a psychologist and learn the
technique of acceptance, but why are they willing to learn it?
Because they are trying to escape from the pain of neurosis,
and we may be sure that in ninety-eight cases out of a hundred, acceptance is simply an indirect method of escape. The
trouble is that a change of technique does not necessarily
involve a change in the person who employs technique. They
alter their tactics, but the fundamental motive remains the
same. You may ask, "Well how do we change our motive?" But
then the answer would be, "Why do you want to change your
motive?" And again we are brought to the admission that our
motive for wanting to change our motive is the same as our
motive for wanting to accept, which, in turn, is the same as
our motive for wanting to escape. I am afraid that is rather a
mouthful, but we are approaching the treacherous ground of
this infinite regression, where everything begins to go crazy.
Thus, we may ask the question in a more general way. Why do
people go in for religion and psychology? Why do they want
to improve themselves? Why do they submit to all manner
of disciplines and techniques to change their attitude to life?
The usual answer is that they wish to achieve some kind of
salvation, some safety and protection from suffering. Herein
is the reason for the popularity of such religious concepts as
personal immortality. This may or may not be a fact; we do
not know, but its vogue arises from its promise of protection

from the alarming prospect of the loss of one's personal self. The same may be said of the general idea of God, especially of the doting mother kind of God we find in the more insipid varieties of Christianity. These are the more obvious forms of spiritual escapism. Less obvious and more subtle are the forms that masquerade as methods of acceptance, which are attempts to escape from the fear of the dark side of life by the purest deception. We are told that we may overcome the fear of life by relaxing to it, but if we relax to it in order to overcome it, we are worse off then we were before; we have simply begun the flight into infinite regression without changing our underlying desire for escape by a single fraction. Beware of the indirect method!

And here, another difficulty arises. We have seen that acceptance is a form of relaxation, which, if it does not come to you naturally, has an awkward habit of eluding you the moment you try to catch it. The reason is that relaxation cannot be achieved by any kind of effort. Mothers are apt to say to excited and sleepless children, "Now dear, try and go to sleep." The poor child tries very hard, but the more they try, the more their tense effort to sleep keeps them awake. Schoolteachers tell children to try to concentrate on a book, a mathematical exercise, or whatever it may be, with the result that in their strenuous attempts to concentrate, their thoughts are completely diverted from the task in hand. They think about themselves trying to concentrate instead of the thing to which they should be attending, and exactly the same difficulty arises in trying to relax psychological tension: your efforts to achieve it stand in your own way. And then, if you try not to try to relax, once more you slip into infinite regression. Thus, the psychology of acceptance is fraught with these two pitfalls, both of which are bottomless, and both of which have a common origin, namely, the desire to escape. On the one hand, if you desire to change this desire, your second desire is only the first once removed; on the other, this desire produces effort, and effort thwarts relaxation. This was clearly recognized by both Buddhists and Taoists of old China. To them, "non-action" was what we call "acceptance." By "non-action," one was supposed to be able to achieve harmony with the Tao, which is their word for the whole of life comprising the two elements of yin and yang, the prototypes of all pairs of opposites. Academic Orientalists often make the ludicrous mistake of equating "non-action" with doing nothing, but these Chinese philosophers and psychologists were much too subtle to imagine that union with the Tao could be had by the deceptive expedient of doing nothing. For to do nothing in order to find the Tao is an indirect way of doing something; and "non-action" has to be much more thoroughgoing than this. Thus, a Buddhist teacher was asked, "What is the Tao?" "Usual life," he replied, "is the Tao." "Well, how do we bring ourselves into accord with it?" "If you *try* to accord with it," was his answer, "you will get away from it."

This brings us to a strange predicament. Acceptance of the opposites and consequent harmony with life is not to be had by trying. Nor is it to be had by a studied not-trying. You cannot get it by doing something about it; you cannot get it by doing nothing about it. At this point, we may be tempted to throw all the books on psychology and religion into the fire, to stop worrying about our mental and spiritual condition, to make an end of listening to lectures and dash for the nearest nightclub. But why do that? If you can't find the Tao in psychology and religion, you won't find it in a nightclub either. For, wherever you look for it, it runs away; and if you try to deceive the devil by pretending to yourself that you are not looking for it, you certainly won't deceive the Tao. It will elude you just as quickly. So, here we are back to the exasperating business of the donkey and the carrot. If the donkey pursues it, it retreats before it; if the donkey does not pursue it, it remains where it is, so near and yet so far.

It is a peculiar problem, and I do not feel that modern psychology has made any really serious attempt to understand it. There is one school that might say that those who find themselves in this predicament should avail themselves of good, healthy wives or husbands wherewith to fulfill the thwarted biological functions whose lack of expression has brought this psychological condition into being. In modern civilization, however, this is not always easy, and even where it is possible, it by no means covers the whole problem. I have a suspicion that psychologists of this school would realize how little their solution contributes if they really fulfilled their own biological functions, for their obsession with such matters seems to indicate a certain rankling lack of experience therein. The Zurich School of Analytical Psychology makes the nearest approach, though it seems to me that Jung himself goes little further than the problem of the *mana* personality. His study of the results of acceptance is both brilliant and profound, but, from the Eastern standpoint, I feel there is something lacking at the very foundations, something without which true acceptance is impossible. At the same time, I do not imagine that analytical psychology could achieve what it has achieved without being able to obtain true acceptance. Even so, I think it must have been obtained somewhat haphazardly, for I know of so many cases of both doctors and laymen, supposed to be completely analyzed, whom I can only describe as psychic ruins. But in this, I am prepared to stand corrected, for Jung and his associates have discovered much that they have never published.

But still, the problem remains to be solved, and I believe that a study of certain forms of Eastern religion is one way of opening our eyes to the solution. It is not the only way, but it seems to me the most convenient. Now I warned you that the solution that they offer may seem quite outrageous, so let us approach it gently on the good principle of "softly, softly, catchee monkey." First, it must be understood that the problem and its solution belong only to one aspect of Eastern religion, an aspect that is most completely expressed in certain Chinese texts compiled between C.E. 500 and the late Middle Ages. Hints of it existed in China as early as 300 B.C.E. in the indigenous religion of Taoism, but it did not reach maturity until the introduction of Buddhism with its traditions of Hindu philosophy, which, together with Taoism, brought the matter to fruition. And here it must be repeated that both the problem and its solution belong purely to what I have described as the spiritual realm, having no necessary connection with that other aspect of Eastern religion, which is yoga, with its cultivation of occult and psychic states.

Both in the Advaita system of the Hindus and in Taoism, there is really only one important doctrine, namely that every possible form of existence is produced by and is itself *brahman* or the Tao. Advaita means literally "not-two," which means to say that there is only one ultimate reality or source of activity in the universe, and as there is only one, nothing can be set in opposition to it. For opposition can arise only when there is duality, and though this one reality expresses itself in innumerable pairs of opposites, there is nothing whatever that can be opposed to the reality itself. So, also, we may say of the Tao that though it is expressed in two opposed (or, from another point of view, complementary) elements—positive and negative, living and dying—there is nothing whatsoever outside the Tao itself. You may think I am talking in the unverifiable abstractions of metaphysics, but that is only because I have used the unfamiliar words *brahman* and Tao. In fact you need no metaphysical knowledge to verify these statements. We often use phrases such as, "Life is like that," or as the French exclaim when things go wrong, *C'est la vie!* If you substitute the word "life" in this wide and all-inclusive sense for *brahman* and Tao, you will begin to understand what these Asian systems mean. The Greeks had a word for it: *To 'ov,* that which is, Being; or, to use Jung's phrase that I have already quoted, it is "what is happening." Life, in this sense, includes all opposites, being a vast conglomeration of people, things, forces, ideas, planets, stars, trees, and houses to the totality of which nothing can be added and from which nothing can be taken away. When Jung was lecturing in London some time ago, he told a story of someone who had asked a Chinese scholar what he meant by Tao. The scholar asked him to look out of the window and tell him what he saw. "*I see* houses and streets," he answered. "What else?" "People are walking about and there are clouds overhead." "What else?" "The wind is blowing." The scholar opened his arms as if to include the whole thing and replied, "That is Tao." And to see it, you do not even have to look out of the window. "Without going out of my house," said Lao-tzu, "I can know the whole universe." For you can find it just by looking into your own mind and watching the inside universe of thoughts and feelings.

But please do not make the mistake of imagining that it needs some special mystical insight to perceive the Tao in and around you. I have said that nothing exists beside or apart from it, and we should not make any opposition between ordinary life (or the world of opposites) and the Tao, as if the Tao were some mysterious essence that lived in the heart of atoms. Chinese philosophers even go so far as to say that when you assert, "Life is Tao," you have made a mistake by trying to join two different concepts that were never in need of joining. Thus, when they are asked about the Tao, they may point at a tree, lift a stick, or smack your face in order to show you, but they do not say that the tree, the stick, or the smack is the Tao, for that would instantly imply a mental division between the two.

What does this mean in terms of psychology? How does it solve the problem of infinite regression? We have said a great deal about this business of escaping from life and accepting it, but all this is based on a false antithesis between ourselves and life. While this antithesis exists, there can be no true acceptance. In fact you cannot escape from life. Civilized people with their acute self-consciousness have always been possessed with the idea that they are in some way out of harmony with life, that they are leading an artificial existence, that they are a lonely orphan divorced from nature, and most of their religion and psychology is so much chattering about this, as some with nothing better to do will chatter about an imaginary illness. Now that we live in cities and everything around us is supposedly artificial, this feeling is increased more than ever. But the Empire State Building is just as much a work of nature as a bird's nest, for though mankind can commit all manner of atrocities, it cannot in any way separate itself from life or the Tao or whatever you like to call it. Try as we may to surround ourselves with so-called artificiality, and try as we may to imagine that we are spiritually distinct and autonomous units, we can worry to the end of time about our lack of harmony with life without ever realizing that this very worrying, this very sense of self-consciousness, is nothing other than the life from which we imagined we were trying to escape. You may escape from unpleasant duties, from unwelcome thoughts and emotions, and from physical and mental pain, up to a point; but from life you can never escape. You can hurl all manner of curses at your fate; you can be the most abominable crybaby; you can fall into infinite regressions by the dozen; you can spend your days looking for salvation, or you can spend them with wine, women, and song. But never in any one of these things do you deny life; for you are life, and life does not deny itself.

This is not just philosophical speculation; it is an understanding of great psychological value, for it gives the most astonishing sense of inner freedom. It means this: that when you are confronted with suffering, you are at liberty to protest and run away as much as you like. If you feel in any way out of harmony with life, you are at liberty to feel out of harmony; you are even at liberty to get worried about it and go to a psychologist. If you want to relax, then relax; if you want to be tense, be tense. If you don't know what you want, you are free to remain in ignorance. Of if you want to do something that the law of the land forbids, you are free to sit down and get mad about being prevented. This is true acceptance, for it is simply allowing yourself to be what it is. Indeed, you could not stop practicing true acceptance even if you wanted to, for your very wanting not to or your very ignorance of the fact that you were doing so is an expression of your true nature. And your true nature always expresses itself, whatever you may think about it, for your true nature is simply life working through your mind and body, and from this there can be no separation, seeing that in all the world there is nothing to be separated from it. We can go so far as to say that even the idea of separation or discord or escape is, as it were, its own idea that you are perfectly free to entertain. What is the therapeutic value of all this? Well, you know what happens when a potential suicide goes to a clever psychologist and threatens to take his own life. The psychologist says, "Go ahead, sir! Who's stopping you? You are quite at liberty to do so, and here is a gun."

I think this may be clarified by expressing it more definitely in religious terms, for these have been coined to provide an easy way of explaining things that are not easily contained within the somewhat elastic significance of ordinary words. The ancient texts say that though all things are the Tao, people imagine that they are separate from it, and so experience a sense of being ill at ease with life. This imagining is the meaning of the familiar Sanskrit word *maya,* or illusion. Hence, to become enlightened, humankind must overcome this illusion and realize unity with the Tao. But, as there is nothing apart from Tao, the illusion must also be Tao, and so must the sense of being ill at ease. Knowing this, a person perceives that they are free to feel separate as much as they like, for they realize that they themselves, with all their thoughts and feelings, are the Tao and that nothing they can think or do can divide them from it. In fact, the whole matter was essentially simple, but they complicated it by trying to catch hold of it when in fact there was nothing to catch hold of. For what they wanted to catch was really themselves, and they spun around in circles to try and see their own eyes instead of looking straight ahead and using them. The Buddhist philosopher Hsuan-chiao expresses it in this way:

Like unto space the Tao knows no boundaries;
Yet it is right here with us, ever retaining its serenity
    and fullness.
It is only when you seek it that you lose it.
You cannot take hold of it, nor can you get rid of it;
While you can do neither, it goes on its own way.
You remain silent and it speaks; you speak and it is silent.

We might add to this that only relatively speaking do you lose it when you seek it; in fact you only seek it because you *think* you have lost it. Thus, in many of the texts, it is said that the only difference between an ordinary man and an enlightened buddha is that one realizes they are a buddha while the other does not. I should explain here that the word "buddha" is used both as the title of an historical person and as the name for the one reality that we may equate with Tao or *brahman*. Thus, in another text we find this from Shih-t'ou:

My teaching which has come down from the ancient buddhas is not dependent on meditation or diligent application of any kind. When you attain insight you know that thoughts are buddha and buddha is thoughts, that thoughts, buddha, sentient beings, enlightenment, and defilements are of one and the same substance while they vary in names.

A pupil once asked, "How does one get emancipated?" The teacher replied, "Who has ever put you in bondage?" In fact, there needs to be nothing done about it at all; you do not have to achieve harmony with life because you already have it; you do not have to reconcile the pairs of opposites, because they are already reconciled. Of course, you may say, it is all very well to put it in so many words, but it is quite another matter to come to the point where you really understand it. In any case, it sounds much too simple to be true, and there must be a snag somewhere. The snag, if any, lies in that odd mental twist that changes the person who doesn't understand into the person who does. But if you let it sink into your mind, the understanding will come one day of its own accord; moreover, everyone is at liberty not to understand, and, if you will forgive the paradox, I would say that one will understand just as soon as they let themself be free to be ignorant, for ignorance also is the Tao.

Therefore, in the end we return to a truth that is both surprising and simple—namely, that our everyday experience is a spiritual experience of the highest order, that union with the Tao is not necessarily a strange state of consciousness nor a particular form of carefully regulated behavior. This truth, to be understood, must first be stood on its head and complicated; in other words, before we can once again feel our unity with the Tao, we must first feel the self-conscious separation from life, which is the peculiar characteristic of civilized people; before we can understand that nothing special has to be done to achieve it we have to go through the psychological process that I have described, undertaking the elusive and irritating task of chasing ourselves and falling into infinite regression through trying to combine things that were never separate. Unless this has been done, the mere statement that ordinary experience is a supreme spiritual experience will be meaningless. Hence, the saying that the aim of religion is to become what you are, or in the words of a Buddhist poem: "This very earth is the Lotus Land of Purity, / And this body is the body of buddha." From the religious point of view, this amounts to the sanctification of all experience. As Thomas á Kempis said, "If thy heart were right, then every creature would be a mirror of life and a book of holy doctrine." From the psychological point of view, it is the acceptance of all experience, and even of those desires and impulses that seem to be the very denial of acceptance. And the joke about genuine acceptance is this: that you do not have to achieve it; you have only to understand that whatever you do or don't do, you cannot get away from it, and this remains true whether you understand it or not.

This state of acceptance or union with the Tao is often described figuratively in Eastern texts as being above and beyond the opposites, as neither good nor evil, living or dying, positive or negative, existent or nonexistent. This means that no affirmative or negative statement can be made concerning it; for the moment you either deny or affirm, something is excluded. That is to say, if you declare, "It is this," you automatically imply, "It is not that," and vice versa, whereas the Tao cannot be limited in this way. And even if we were to say that the Tao excludes nothing, this too would be a limitation. But if this is getting too metaphysical, let me round off the argument with a story that demonstrates the matter in a more practical way. A Chinese sage was asked the same pressing question, "It is terribly hot, and how shall we escape the heat?" He replied, "Why not go to the place where it is neither hot nor cold?" Again he was asked, "But where is the place where it is neither hot nor cold?" "When it is hot," he answered, "we go to the stream by the bamboo grove. When it is cold we gather round the fire." You can take that story in a number of ways, substituting any pair of opposites and their appropriate reactions for heat and cold.

When this understanding matures in the right time and place, its psychological effects are astonishing, for it creates an inner freedom and spontaneity, a sense of being at ease in the world and at home with the demons of one's own mind that has to be felt to be believed. There are problems that it does not solve, for these are problems of a different order— moral, social, medical, economic, and political. It gives a new zest for approaching these problems, but in itself it is purely a matter of psychological adjustment, of spiritual ease and dis-ease, giving us the power to devote ourselves joyously and unreservedly to the technical problems of life without cherishing any private hopes or fears as to whether we are saved or damned, or as to whether this or that is going to make us happy or miserable. You may object that it is a peculiarly dangerous and irresponsible doctrine. This is perfectly true, so perhaps you had better not tell anyone about it when you go away, for it has been systematically hushed-up in almost every form of religion for thousands of years. Wherever it was actually taught it was handled, as it were, with the rubber gloves and forceps of a rigid moral discipline, lest anyone should imagine that it gave them freedom to behave just as they pleased. For from one point of view, it is a neutral force, which, like electricity, may either slay or heal, and, as with electricity, there is a price to be paid for its misuse. If it were proclaimed from the housetops, there would undoubtedly be trouble, but, if we are to judge from the history of the religions wherein it has been understood, its effect on a reasonably balanced mind is to produce a reverence and respect for life that does not encourage abuse. For it enables you to understand that your own antisocial desires may be at once accepted and denied, seeing that neither self-indulgence nor self-denial are contrary to true acceptance. But more than this: if evil and crime arise from the hatred of life, from a fundamental antagonism to the world, hatred becomes very dull when you know you are free to hate as much as you like; it becomes ashamed of itself like the fractious, squawking child whose mother says to it, "That's right dear, have a good cry. Go on, scream, lie on the floor, kick your legs. Don't worry if the neighbors hear. Have a good yell." This antagonism, in one or another of its many forms, is at the root of crime and religious endeavor alike, for fundamentally it is the sense of opposition between oneself and the world. Given recognition and free rein, it becomes absurd, and you realize also that whatever in fact you do or don't do, you are capable of and free to do almost anything that is humanly possible, whether supreme virtue or abysmal crime. A story is told of a Tibetan Buddhist teacher examining a disciple prior to initiation. On being asked whether he could tell a lie, the disciple was profoundly shocked, and replied that it was of course impossible for him to commit such a violation of the precepts. "Well then," said the teacher, "go away and learn how to tell a lie, and until you have learnt, don't come back to me for initiation." For the knowledge that you are capable of anything in this sense at once creates a new and more harmonious relation with the world of men, a relation that might be expressed in those two old sayings *Tout comprendre c'est tout pardonner,* and *Humani nihil a me alienum puto:* I think myself estranged to nothing human.

But there is more to it than this. For the understanding that ordinary experience is a supreme spiritual experience has an effect that is best described as a feeling of wonder for life in which there is something childlike, whereof we may say, "Of such is the kingdom of Heaven." A Chinese poet expressed it in this way:

How wondrously supernatural,
And how miraculous this—
I draw water and I carry fuel!

The sense of being at ease with the world leaves one free to contemplate and enjoy things that the terribly serious and earnestly seeking religious state of mind considers too trivial. People whose minds are in this condition are so taken up with "the Search" that they have neither the time nor the taste for ordinary human pursuits. They enjoy no other conversation than that of the "higher things," and find it so hard to unbend, to chatter about nothing in particular for the sake of being sociable, to roll about on the floor and play with children, to go about and gape at wonderful things, at landscapes, waterfalls, crowds, circuses, thunderstorms, and curious people, to enjoy a good dinner, to lie on one's back in the sun and think about nothing except chewing a piece of grass, to sing, dance, tell stories, or to stroll aimlessly around Central Park in the evening, watching the lights of the big city. Spiritual insight reveals a mystery and magic in these things that no one should be ashamed to feel.

It has been said that the mystery of life is not a problem to be solved, but a reality to be experienced, and when certain scientists claim that they are on the way to banishing all mysteries, to explaining everything in the universe, they should also realize that they are on their way to explaining the universe away. But if I am to say just how the magic gets into these ordinary things of life, you must excuse my being slightly poetical, for no other mode of expression quite conveys the feeling. The magic of life is in the fact that every littlest thing, both in and around you, expresses, and in action uses, the same power that hurls the stars through space and causes their fire; that bellows in thunder and whispers in wind; that produces a giant tree from the microscopic germ of a seed and wears away mountains to thin clouds of dust. It is in the fact that whatever you feel, think, do, or say, you cannot cut yourself off from it; in spite of all your mistakes, in spite of all your imaginings and fears, never for a moment do you cease to use and share in its tremendous freedom. To exist, it must include all opposites, and hence can suffer from none of them; thus, you express it in living as much as in dying, in creating as much as in destroying, in accepting as much as in escaping, in being wise as much as in being a fool. Therefore, when the *mana* personality rears its subtle head and a person becomes inflated with the conceit of themself as a spiritual giant who has accepted all life and reconciled the opposites, let them remember that life was never in need of being accepted nor the opposites of being reconciled. Worms, skunks, morons, and drunkards are in fact accepting it as much as we, and the only difference is that we know it while they do not. But that we have at last discovered it is less a cause for pride than for laughter at ourselves for not having seen it before.

Mythological Motifs
in Modern Science

A Chinese poem says human life is "Like a sword that cuts, but cannot cut itself; Like an eye that sees, but cannot see itself."

In short, our predicament is that we cannot at one and the same time be subject and object, observer and observed, controller and controlled. This is another way of saying that the inner origins of our thought and action must always be unconscious. However much we may understand ourselves, the very act of understanding alters what we understand, and to explore human nature is to change it in unpredictable ways so that, to some extent, our knowledge of ourselves is always obsolete. If this be true, it will also be true that humankind must always be makers of myth. For, as I understand it, myth is the imagery whereby we project upon the known, external world the ever-changing and ungraspable pattern of our own unconscious and inner workings.

The whole psychology of the unconscious, deriving from the work of Freud and Jung, has, I believe, established the fact that our view of the world, our theology or cosmology, is always the external projection of processes within ourselves that are otherwise unknown. But I do not believe that it has been able to prove that these processes are as invariable and common to all as their physical structure. A universal and definitive science of the unconscious is really a contradiction in terms, for the whole value of the idea of the unconscious is not that it opens up a new realm of the world to be explored and mastered but rather that it points out the elastic though nonetheless inescapable limitations of consciousness and of its ability to control both itself and the surrounding world.

To a very important extent, science is a Western attempt to liberate oneself from myth, from the so-called "pathetic fallacy" of constructing the world in our own unconscious image. Without detracting from the glory of science, I want to suggest that this attempt is impossible and absurd, and I will do so by discussing the parallel between Western science and Eastern efforts to achieve the same objective along other lines. Here I should say that I am approaching this subject not so much as a historian or philosopher of science, but as a student of the comparative philosophies of Asia and the West.

There is an old Indian tale of a king who lived in the far-off times when people walked barefooted upon this stony and rugged earth, and who proposed one day that thousands of cattle should be slain so that the ground might be covered with their skins. However, a philosopher at his court suggested that if only a few cattle were slain, small pieces of their hide might be bound to people's feet so that a carpet of leather would, in effect, be available wherever they want. This story is a parable of the differing ways in which Western and Eastern cultures have, in general, approached the problem of controlling what we experience so as to reduce suffering. The West, covering the whole ground with skins, has invented the technology of mastering the external world. The East, putting mere strips of leather on the feet, has neglected the external world and idealized the control of the mind. It has concentrated upon solving the problem by changing oneself rather than the environment, and the success and failure of both attempts are enormously instructive.

The cultures of India and China have invented their own techniques of liberation from myth. Anyone who is set upon overcoming myth will use the word in its pejorative sense to mean "falsehood" or "illusion" as opposed to "truth" and "fact." It is in this sense that the Hindu and Buddhist philosophies of India frequently use the word *maya* to suggest that the external world, or perhaps the way in which we think about the world, is an illusion arising in our own minds. So long as this illusion arises, life in the world appears to be painful and problematic. But if the mind can be controlled so that the illusion ceases, the hard world, or perhaps just our objections to it, will vanish.

Let us first consider the cosmology, the view of the world, largely common to both Hinduism and Buddhism—or rather to the culture in which they arose as ways of liberation from that cosmology. Every life, whether human or animal, angelic or demonic, is seen as a link in an inconceivably long series of incarnations through which every individualized being must pass so long as they feel themself to be an individual. The series of incarnations is not so much a progressive evolution as a cycle of slow alternation between the good and the evil, the zenith of the angelic paradises of the *devas* and the nadir of hideous purgatories of the *narakas;* existence is an everlasting to-and-fro of pleasure and pain inseparably linked by the logic of their polarity, measured in periods of the *kalpa,* a unit of 4,320,000 years. So long as the being is in the grip of *karma,* the process of conditioned action regulated by attraction and repulsion, they will rotate indefinitely within this cycle for *kalpa* after *kalpa.* The whole scheme is in fact a cosmic squirrel-cage treadmill of vast proportions, kept in motion by the pursuit of pleasure in all its forms, physical and spiritual.

Yet, to Hinduism and Buddhism alike, this cosmology, as well as the individual beings in its toils, is *maya* (a myth, projection, or illusion arising within the mind) as a consequence of *avidya* ("ignorance" or "unconsciousness"). *Avidya* is a word of many meanings. It may signify forgetfulness of the fact that one's consciousness is not individual and separate, but a ray of the *atman,* the divine Self that is the one and only reality. It may mean failure to see that pleasure and pain, good and evil, are correlative and that therefore the search for one creates the other as surely as height implies depth. It may also be taken in the special sense of "ignore-ance." This is the use of consciousness for selective attention, the act of focusing the mind upon limited areas of the world one after another so as to ignore its unity and create the impression that it is a multiplicity of distinct things and events. *Avidya* is therefore the unconsciousness, the "screening-out" of the truth that all things and all events and their polarities are inseparably related, and that there is therefore no way of disentangling the "I" from the "thou" or of wresting the desirable from the undesirable.

It follows, then, that control and mastery of the cosmic squirrel-cage treadmill must come about through control and mastery of the mind and the overcoming of *avidya*. By the disciplines of yoga, the mind must be stilled and concentrated. It is then turned back upon itself through the gates of the senses so as to withdraw the projection of an external world, and finally of the sense-gates themselves, the body, and the individualized consciousness. To us this may seem as fantastic as crawling into a hole and pulling the hole in after us, or as unrealistic as playing ostrich. Nevertheless, there is something in it, for we know that the appearance of the external world is relative to the structure of our brains and sense organs. If these can be changed, the world can be changed, at least for the individual undertaking the task. They are the one with sandals in a barefooted society. According to your prejudices, you may call them a victim of hallucination or the discoverer of a new level of reality, the first of a new type of person. The fact that the vast majority of people see the world in the same way does not mean that they are right: it means simply that they are in communication and that they are structures of the same kind.

But to at least one major school of Asian philosophy, this way of overcoming *maya*, and thus of controlling the world, did not seem at all satisfactory. On the contrary, the general consensus of Mahayana Buddhism was that the attempt to obliterate *maya* and gain total control of unconscious projection was to become the victim of illusion in a peculiarly deep and tragic way. For this school, the term *pratyeka-buddha*, meaning originally "one who passes into *nirvana* without staying in communication with other people," became a term of opprobrium. In most of the Mahayana texts, the *pratyekabuddha*, or "private buddha," is not a buddha at all. For, in withdrawing into spiritual isolation and in damming up the projection of *maya* entirely, they fail to realize that they have become its most pitiful slave, myth-bound in the worst sense. It is here that we shall find a parallel with the dark or maleficent role of myth in modern science.

Now the predicament of the *pratyeka-buddha*, or of the *yogi* who has gained total control of their mind, is not unlike that of the absolute ruler described in that classical manual of Indian politics, the *Arthashastra*. Here, the tyrant-king is depicted as governing the *mandala*, or concentric circles, of his subordinates like a spider in the midst of a web. On the principle of *divide et impera*, each ring of subordinates is set in mistrust of its neighboring ring so that adjacent ranks are always spying upon each other. The immediate guards or ministers of the king are watched by their next inferiors, jealous of their position and ever ready to seek favor and promotion by betraying them to the monarch and so on all down the hierarchy from the chief ministers to the slaves. And, because the whole system is a clever balancing of mutual mistrust, the king himself, the final guardian of his own guards, can trust no one at all. He must even sleep with one eye open, and never, never give himself the luxury of rest from vigilance. But this means only that the ruler of the system is himself its most total prisoner, the spider caught in its own web. So, too, the secret police in Orwell's *1984* must sit and watch the innumerable television screens that bug the citizens' homes, glued by their eyes to the task of mistrust instead of being able to go walking with their girls in the park.

The development of Mahayana Buddhism arose, then, from the recognition that complete self-consciousness and self-control are also complete self-frustration, the frustration of the sword trying to cut itself, or, as we would say, of trying to lift oneself up by one's own bootstraps. In technical terms, the delusion of the *pratyeka-buddha* is that *nirvana,* the state of liberation, is something apart from *samsara,* the cycle of birth and death generated by *maya.* If *nirvana* is to be understood as withdrawal from the world, as getting away from sense-experience so as to be in a position to master it, this is equivalent to the idea that the controlling self or subject is in fact separate from what it controls. This, however, is to be unaware of the fact that the controlling will *also* is *maya,* or, as we might say, that the human brain is part of its own environment. To seek to know the unconscious down to its depths is to forget that it is the unconscious itself that sees, that consciousness is not apart from the unconscious, but is one of its functions: "Like an eye that sees, but cannot see itself."

It is thus that the bodhisattva, the ideal person of Mahayana Buddhism, is represented as one who, after withdrawal, returns into the world out of compassion for "all sentient beings," vowing not to enter *nirvana* until all others are delivered with them. But their compassion for sentient beings arises from the discovery that they are inseparable from them. What the bodhisattva has really found out is that there is no escape from the world, because there is no one to escape from it. They see that other sentient beings are suffering just because they think that they are separate and are trying in innumerable ways to get out of a trap in which no one is caught, because there is *only* the trap. No flies at all! The classical expression of this is the passage in the *Lankavatara Sutra,* which says:

> Those who, afraid of the sufferings arising from the discrimination of birth-and-death (*samsara*), seek for *nirvana,* do not know that birth-and-death and *nirvana* are not to be separated from one another . . . imagining that *nirvana* consists in the future annihilation of the senses and their fields. (II. 18.)

Or again, the words of the Chinese Mahayanist Seng-ts'an:

> Don't be antagonistic to the world of the senses,
> For when you are not antagonistic to it,
> It turns out to be the same as complete Awakening.

The wise person does not strive;
The ignorant man ties himself up.
(For) if you work on your mind with your mind,
How can you avoid an immense confusion?

At this point, the movement of Indian philosophy seems to have completed a cycle that was always implied in what is probably the basic myth of Hinduism: that all living beings are the dreams of God, innumerable parts played by the one divine Actor, who, just because he is omnipotent and omniscient, can afford the game of plunging himself into illusion. Thus as soon as the slumbering Self, the *atman*, awakens from the dream of *maya*, it discovers that all the figures of the dream are not its antagonists, but its own will. And God, like his own saints, is divine in the act of giving up his will, in the act of what Eastern Christianity calls *kenosis*, the self-emptying or self-surrender of the Godhead whereby he both creates the world and becomes incarnate in the Son of Man. I do not know whether this is true of God, but certainly it was the discovery of the Mahayana philosophers that when the mind's experience is perfectly controlled it is no longer worth controlling. *Nirvana* therefore becomes the freedom to embrace the world, to deliver oneself over to love and attachment, and to will one's own involvement in *maya*.

Western science is also a way of liberation, but thus far it has proceeded in a different direction to the same goal of controlling the content of our experience, concentrating upon the transformation and understanding of the external world. In

its own way, science has also been concerned with the dissolution of *maya* and has delivered multitudes from the terrors of
a cosmology not of endless reincarnation but of the last judgment, Heaven, and Hell. Yet its method of attack is, at first
sight, quite different, for it did not take as a point of depar-
ture the equation of *maya* with the physical world. For science,
maya is not nature but ideas about nature based upon precon-
ception rather than observed fact. Ignorance, furthermore, is
not as in Indian thought the perception of the world as a multiplicity of facts, but precisely ignorance *of* facts. Science did
not, therefore, dissolve the Ptolemaic-Christian cosmology by
discovering it to be a mental projection upon the void, but by
discovering it to be an inadequate explanation of astronomi-
cal facts. The cosmology was a myth and a projection indeed;
but it was not so much this that made it false as that it did not
fit the observable form of the screen.

For the scientist, too, projects. His or her scales and
hypotheses are all projections of human thought upon the
world. But they know them to be projections, and it is their
claim that they are not projecting unconsciously. Ancient
astronomers found their way among the stars by associat-
ing their apparent groupings with such concrete images as
the signs of the zodiac. Their belief in astrological influences
suggests that they did not realize either that they were projecting these images or that the constellations to which
they were assigned were groupings selected by mere convenience. They may have had no inkling that they were treating
the heavens as an immense Rorschach blot, seeing forms in

the stars according to their inner psychic disposition, which had been given collective coherence by the matrix of social tradition and convention. But the modern astronomer finds it more accurate and serviceable to chart the position of the stars upon an abstract grid of sidereal latitude and longitude, knowing perfectly well that the grid is a projection that does not actually hang in the sky.

If, then, scientific projection is always conscious and if the scientist is more and more aware that they are describing the world in terms of measures that they have themself invented, will they not be the last person to confuse these measures with the world? Is not science precisely an anti-mythology in which, as time goes on, we shall seek in vain for any unconscious image? Today scientists are so conscious and critical of their own methods and procedures, and have gone so far in the controlled analysis of scientific thinking itself, that Western man's concern for the control of nature is slipping over into Eastern man's concern for controlling the mind. We are now beginning to attack *maya* in both directions, and for this reason books on the philosophy of science become more and more reminiscent of Indian metaphysics; I am not thinking simply of Eddington and Schrödinger but also of Mach, Wittgenstein, and Schlick, and the whole school of thought that Popper calls "instrumentalist." In the present century the vestiges of myth have been disappearing from science with ever increasing rapidity. Yet as they do so they reappear with greater force than ever in an unsuspected, and thus unconscious, direction.

The worldview of science might still have contained something mythical when, say, a scientist of the eighteenth century could have been astonished to find that the tossing of dice "obeyed" the laws of probability. They could have believed that, after all, there was some sort of objective design or law out there in the universe, and that God or nature was inherently mathematical. But today, we are as reluctant to speak of events as "obeying" laws as to say that some trees have winged seeds "in order" to scatter them on the wind. We tend now to think of natural laws as inventions or instruments, like the decimal system of numbering. The misnamed "laws" of probability are thus a mathematical invention, like the ruler, convenient for measuring large numbers of events, which, when taken in small numbers, are highly irregular. Events do not follow laws, for what we call laws are now seen to be patterns that we have constructed for predicting events just as we have constructed combs for arranging our hair. God did not make hair so as to fit combs any more than God made noses to support spectacles.

As the scientific naturalism of the nineteenth century abandoned the theological hypothesis, or myth, of the divine lawgiver behind the laws, the scientific instrumentalism of the twentieth century is abandoning the laws. Even that myth is going, and the realization that laws are *maya* is being swiftly followed by the realization that even facts, yes, those precious "scientific facts" are *maya*. We are seeing that the fact, the thing, or the event is a useful unit of thought, but that there are no formally separate entities in the physical world. Certainly, the external world contains clear divisions and lines, patterns, and structures, but the way we gather them into units or things or facts is as conventional as our perception of constellations among the stars. As de Chardin has put it:

> It is time to point out that this procedure is merely an intellectual dodge. Considered in its physical, concrete reality, the stuff of the universe cannot divide itself, but, as a kind of gigantic "atom" it forms in its totality . . . the only real indivisible. . . . It is impossible to cut into this network, to isolate a portion without it becoming frayed and unravelled at all its edges. All around us, as far as the eye can see, the universe holds together, and only one way of considering it is really possible—that is, to take it as a whole, in one piece.

It is convenient to think of the world in terms of things just as it is convenient to carve up a chicken for eating. But "cut-up broilers" do not emerge from the egg.

But what is happening here? If the laws and even the facts of nature are our own conceptual constructions, rooted ever more in conscious rationality alone, must we not feel increasingly estranged from the actual world outside our brains? Consider for a moment the situation in applied science and technology. The great scientific revolution of the nineteenth century was pervaded by a philosophy of naturalistic or materialistic monism that, in theory, was opposed to the traditional Western and Christian dualism of spirit and matter, soul and body. Freud, Haeckel, and Huxley were sure that all phenomena of the psyche could be explained in terms of the body, that one need no longer be considered a duality, a conscious spiritual will in control, chauffeur-wise, of a physical vehicle. Now one might have thought that this unitary view of nature would have done something to reduce Western culture's strong sense of alienation and separation from the physical environment. But, on the contrary, scientific naturalism gave rise to a technology that we commonly call "the conquest of nature."

The theory of our spontaneous evolution out of the natural order has issued in the feeling that the "blind" processes of this order can no longer be trusted, and that the future development of the world must be by the indefinite increase of conscious control. This point of view is not only paradoxical, but also absurd, when one considers that the brain through which such control is exercised is itself a product of spontaneous process and is organized so complexly that our conscious, scientific understanding of it is still rudimentary. It seems, then, that science, so far from overcoming the myth of the dualistic universe, has exaggerated it to an enormous degree. Humanity and nature, reason and instinct, calculation and spontaneity are now in practice more widely sundered than ever.

The modern counterpart of the traditional Christian urge to subordinate nature rigorously to the law of God is the technological ambition of rendering all nature, human and subhuman, an object of rational control. Is not technology in a direct line of descent from the Christian fascination for miracles, for spiritual power that proves itself precisely in transforming the hard material world? Though it is not stated in overtly supernatural terms, we are still in practice devotees of the faith that proves itself by moving mountains and resurrecting the dead. The flesh with its finite limitations is still our enemy, and its failure to respond to our control is still the work of the devil. Surely, too, there is more than a touch of ascetic spirituality in the fact that the image in which physicists conceive the world has less and less resemblance to any form of sensuous imagery. Scientific knowledge, says Oppenheimer "has become the property of specialized communities who pursue their own way with growing intensity further and further from their roots in ordinary life."

Yet, as always, miracles alone turn out to be empty victories. In the first place, it has become obvious to us that the miracles that we perform through physics and chemistry are disastrous in the hands of insane, stupid, or malicious people. Science cannot rest content with the control of external nature: through sociology, psychology, and psychiatry, technology must be extended into people themselves so that we can control the controller. But here, in the second place, the victory is empty again, for like the *pratyeka-buddha,* the controller who approaches perfect control of themselves is locked in a vicious circle in which action is increasingly paralyzed. The growth of bureaucracy, conformism, and regimentation in our society is not the result of some dark conspiracy but of the simple logic of regulating the behavior of people who handle such dangerous instruments as electricity, automobiles, airplanes, and nuclear power. So long, then, as our objective is the miracle, power and control over ourselves and the world, our society must come to resemble the *mandala-trap* of the *Arthashastra*, only in the modern version of the totalitarian state, the system of mutual mistrust in which every person is their neighbor's policeman. And here the game is not worth the candle. The price of omnipotence, of possessing the powers of the dictator-God, is to be strangled in the network of one's own controls.

In this light, let us look again at the patterns that our modern wisdom projects upon Heaven and Earth, ostensibly in full rational consciousness, but practically unaware of the inseparability of reason and nature, and therefore, as Jung would say, under the spell of the mythological archetype of the supernatural, purely spiritual, and omnipotent God. Certainly, the formal net of celestial latitude and longitude is very convenient, as are the grid-iron streets of Chicago as compared with those of Boston and London (except when they are laid down in such defiance of topography as upon the hills of San Francisco). But such convenience *is* convenient from the standpoint of a mentality that would control the world rather than love it, and when it is in this spirit that we cover the world with reticulations of numbered pattern, the convenience that we intended turns out to be the myth that we did not intend. Oppenheimer has spoken of science as "the things we have discovered about nature defined in terms of the ways in which they were found out." The ways include both the specific techniques and the motivation behind them, and when this is the network of conceptual abstractions projected upon nature for no other reason than to master it, nature somehow vanishes and we are left with the net. We are left, that is, with a conception of the world in which there seems to be no order except what humankind imposes upon it, and thus a world that is in itself completely foreign to us. And because we come to feel nature in the ways that we define it, we are left with nothing to control or to experience except the systems of control whereby nature has been defined. The social parallel is that highly mechanized cultures begin to serve the logic of machines rather than the desires of people.

Naturalistic monism to the contrary, Western science—save with certain exceptions yet to be mentioned—has not actually realized that humanity is inseparable from their environment. If we draw the conclusion that the order of nature is no more than its description in terms of our calculus, and that therefore the pattern of the world is simply the invention of human consciousness, we are talking as if human consciousness were not part of the world. The solid objection to all purely instrumentalist theories of natural order is that consciousness and its functions—reason, observation, and calculation—are not inventions of consciousness. They are operations of a cerebral cortex that is part of its own environment, and that grew out of that environment without first intending to do so.

The pretension of consciousness is that it can become its own object, that is, stand outside itself and the world of which it is a part. But as [Perry Williams] Bridgman has put it, "the insight that we can never get away from ourselves is an insight that the human race through its long history has been deliberately—one is tempted to say wilfully—refusing to admit." The mathematical analogue is the Gödel theorem that no system can be shown to be without contradiction except in terms of a higher system, so that one may pile up systems and meta-systems forever without attaining the point beyond doubt. To put the same thing in terms of Indian philosophy, nothing entraps one so deeply in *maya* as the attempt to get out of it. Nothing is so unconscious as the ambition to be completely conscious. As Shankara himself said of the Godhead, the Brahman, "It is the knower, and the knower can know other things, but cannot make itself the object of its own knowledge, in the same way that fire can burn other things but cannot burn itself."

Thus if we think we have a purely rational, conscious, and unmythical picture of nature in terms of the scientific calculus, what we have in fact is the very image of *maya* in its most primordial form. For *maya* in its root form *ma* means "to measure," and its inflection *matr-* gives us "meter," "matrix," and perhaps "material." In standing back to see the world quite objectively, therefore, we find ourselves caught in the primal image of illusion, the entangling web of *maya* as the spider mother who sucks the life from us.

All this is anything but a diatribe against the pursuit of science. If science is in any sense a sin, I would say, *"Peccate fortiter!"* It is through the full and exhaustive following of science that we discover the dimensions and rationale of the trap in which our consciousness involves itself when it aspires to too great a control of itself and the world. The limits of control are already being explored and clarified in the cybernetics of Norbert Wiener. The inseparability of humanity and nature becomes evident with an altogether new lucidity with every step in ecology. In psychiatry and psychology, where technology reaches most deeply into a person, there have long been those who have insisted upon the healing power of a basic trust in the unconscious. But what interests me most is the growing success of people engaged in basic research in persuading government and industry that nothing of any consequence will be discovered unless scientists are allowed to be playful, unscheduled, and whimsical. Here the whole process is at last in reverse, for the need for more and more science produces the need for more and more spontaneous, playful, and unpredictable people in white coats. Certainly, *more* playfulness will not produce scientific discovery, nor any other kind of valuable creation. Yet rigorous discipline and exact thinking must always be subordinate to the whimsical unconscious; subordinate, but nevertheless its indispensable tools.

The whole situation of science today is profoundly mythological, since it is a reenactment of basic themes in the mythologies of God. As yet, perhaps, it is no more than science fiction, but the logical goal of technology is a world in which the touch of a button will grant every desire, and where desires themselves will be made desirable desires by the proper drugs or alterations of the brain. But such a world would swiftly become intolerable without the introduction of a button labeled "Surprise!" At first, pleasant surprises; later, some nasty ones to add a certain spice and adventure to experience. It is thus that in the *Kalika Purana*, Brahma is sunk in deep meditation at the beginning of the worlds, when—whoops!—out of the depths of his being there emerges the youth called Love, to the total astonishment and disquiet of the Creator. There is rather the same feeling in Genesis where it is said, without any apparent forethought or reason, "And God created great whales. . ." Just like that, and only afterward did he look and see that it was good. If, then, the very omnipotence that creates the worlds is God letting go of himself, is not science with all the techniques and disciplines now at its disposal, able to set aside being so largely practical and useful and let fantasy bring far greater wonders from the mind than giant rockets and huge explosions?

Time and Convention

Five Broadcasts

1. Time and the Moment

It's very difficult to enter deeply into the feelings of people among whom you were not born and brought up. Thus I am not quite sure whether Americans have the same peculiar sensations about a Sunday evening that I felt as a child in England. I think there is probably some difference, because in American cities there is not quite the same Sunday atmosphere of utterly rolled-up sidewalks, of Saturday night's dinner warmed over for supper, of a kind of respectably religious depression hanging over from times when Sunday was the Lord's Day, with a vengeance. In this country we do not have quite the same intolerable sadness of streets echoing with church bells ringing for Evensong, nor the same association of the ending of the day with the ending of life—with hell beyond the grave, or worse, the everlasting hymn-singing of a churchly heaven. But here, too, I believe that Sunday evenings bring for many of us a kind of letdown of the spirits, as we are aware of the approaching Monday morning and another week of work ahead. In a culture where work is so strictly divided from play, one does not want the vacation to end, and at the end of a period of rest and play you might want to say with the Latin poet, "O *lente, lente currite noctis equi!* "—"O slowly, slowly run, ye horses of the night!" Let time slow down, and the party with beer and coffee round the fire not come to an end.

Since childhood, and since coming to this country, I am happy to say that this peculiar Sunday evening feeling has almost entirely left me. But there does remain, at about this time of night, a sense of the slowing down of time, as if somewhere between now and the dawn one approached an interval through which one might slip out of time altogether; a pause of the minute hand in which the world may be seen, even for a long moment, from the standpoint of eternity. In a day when time is money and money is value, this is not a fashionable standpoint. It is equally unfashionable for those to whom time is not money but opportunity, and progress toward insufferably busy ideals. All of this, as I see it, leads to a frightful impoverishment of life, to a routine of witless activity in which there is no pause for wonder.

I am simply appalled by the number of my acquaintances for whom any sort of play of the imagination, any release from dogged practicality or from the hectic pursuit of pleasure or culture, seems impossible. For those who feel this way, a slowing down of time is simply boredom—an occasion to yawn or look for a more or less violent distraction. But there are others for whom this is not so—for whom the slow moments of time are the most valuable, since they are, as it were, chinks through which the world is seen clearly, through which one is able to contemplate the beautiful and terrible fascination of what *is,* instead of chasing the comparatively vapid and stereotyped visions of what *ought* to be. Therefore, as Sunday evening is one of these slow times, I thought that some of you might enjoy it as an occasion for speculation—in the original sense of the speculum or mirror, the instrument of reflection—for simply wondering at and about the course of our life.

For this has always seemed to me the proper activity of philosophy and religion. Yet these are almost hateful terms to those who think of philosophy as an academic splitting of hairs, and of religion as a stuffy moralism or a literalistic mythology. To me, philosophy and religion have always been ways of expressing the sense that being alive is uncanny and strange; and thus it has seemed utterly incomprehensible that there are people for whom they are of no interest. I really don't believe that there are such people. One can very read-ily sympathize with those for whom textbook philosophy and conventional religion are a bore, but surely they must express their feeling of wonder in other ways, calling it by other names, such as science or art, or by no names at all.

I think, then, we might begin with what to many of us must seem the queerest of all queer things—our sense of living in a one-way oddity called Time, of being involved in a movement that never stops and that never goes back on its course. Scientifically speaking, time is a measurement of motion in space—the standard of measurement being the rotation of the earth upon its own axis and about the sun. By these we set our clocks, with their evenly spaced cogs and their regularly divided circular dials—in the simple and very trusting faith that the speed of the earth is constant, that it does not go faster some days and slower on others. Of course the clocks tell us that all days go past at the same speed, despite the vivid subjective feeling that some days rush and some simply drag. For in addition to clock time there is also biological and psychological time—measured, no doubt, by less constant processes than the rotation of the earth, processes such as metabolism, the beat of the heart, and the rhythm of the lungs. Incidentally, it has often seemed to me that these biological processes are much more fundamental to humanity than the rotation of the earth, and I have wondered whether we might not construct a more congenially shaped clock, elliptical, ovoid, or perhaps Mae Westish in form to be in time with the rhythms of a more subtle organism than a planet.

But I think we may agree without further argument that time is a measure of motion, and that the problem of time is really the problem of motion. To wonder what time is, is really to wonder what motion is. In all probability this is one of those problems that seem to be made for wondering rather than answering, and I am not going to attempt to make any definition of motion. But this much we *can* say: that all motion is relative—meaning that nothing can be said to be moving except in relation to something else that is relatively still. We *know* that the earth is rotating only because of the apparent movement of the sun and the stars. If the earth were the only object in space, we should not be able to determine whether it was moving, since there would be no relatively stable objects to give points of comparison.

The question then arises: under such circumstances, would the earth be moving in reality without our being able to notice it? Would the earth be moving if all other planets, stars, and galaxies were suddenly to vanish? I find it quite fascinating to realize that this question has no answer, not because we do not know, but because it is perfectly meaningless. For if there were no other objects in space than the earth itself, there would be nothing whatsoever with respect to which the earth could be said to be moving—toward it, away from it, or around it. Motion is a property that does not come into play unless there are, at the very least, two bodies: and though we can't go into it very deeply at the moment, this is true of other things besides motion. It is also true of facts, things, or events: it is quite impossible to conceive a single, solitary fact without at least one other fact. Just try to visualize a simple image without any background!

To say, then, that motion and time are relative is to say that there is no absolute motion. But this is also to say that there is no absolute stillness—because the relationship of motion and stillness is mutual. If we perceive motion be comparative stillness, we perceive stillness by comparative motion. It would therefore be a mistake to suppose that either the earth all by itself or the sum total of bodies in space—whichever you please—is absolutely still because it has no absolute motion. For we are speaking of a situation in which the concepts of motion and stillness are simply inapplicable and meaningless.

To come back to earth, I have already noted other ways in which we perceive the relativity of motion and time—the psychological sensations of time flying and time dragging. Try the experiment of watching the sweep hand on an electric clock. By a simple adjustment of your imagination you can feel that hand either as rushing around the clock or as crawling around it. You can think of time as the earth turning upon its axis at almost one thousand miles per hour, or as the sun creeping across the sky so slowly that you can hardly notice it. Close your eyes, and think of yourself as living on through time—moving continuously from the past into the future. How fast are you going? Are you sailing with a gentle wind or going by jet propulsion? You will find that you can adjust your sensations equally well to either image. And now comes a very interesting question: how slow a sensation of time can you get? Change from jet propulsion to sail. Any image will do, provided that it is something that moves continuously, without jerks. Now change from sail to snail? Perhaps the hour hand of a clock. Obviously we can get slower than that—much slower—and yet still be moving continuously. How slow can slow be?

I wonder—what is the effect of slowing down your image of the passage of time? Does it make you feel rested—or simply impatient? Just for the sake of experiment, you might try the reverse process: speeding up the image, thinking of yourself hurtling through time at the speed of light, or at the speed of thought, which can jump in a single instant to the remotest galaxies. With such a very fast image in mind, it may seem to you that the ordinary events around you are taking place extremely slowly. Whereas, on the other hand, a slow snail's pace image of time may make it seem that events are rushing past you and leaving you way behind. But the point I want to make is this: that all these images are attempts to visualize the speed of the absolute time at which you are moving from past to future, to find some figure of the rate at which your lifetime is "really" passing. But, you see, you can think of it any way you please—as fast as you like or as slow as you like. So I might paraphrase Shakespeare and say, "There is nothing either slow or fast, but thinking makes it so."

There is a story that somewhere around 1400, the abbot of a Benedictine monastery in Germany, whose name was John, went for a walk by himself to the top of a hill near the monastery. High in the air above the hill's crown there was a skylark, bouncing up and down, and singing so rapturously that the abbot was caught up into an ecstasy—and for an intense moment lived in eternity, listening to the hymns of the six-winged cherubim and seraphim as they danced in flight at the very center of the light of God. The vision passed, and the abbot returned to the monastery. At the gatehouse a surprised and unfamiliar monk opened the wicket and asked the abbot his name and his business. "What do you mean!" exclaimed the abbot. "I am your Abbot John, and I have just been out for a walk." "Abbot John!" said the gatekeeper. There is no abbot John here. Our abbot's name is Gregory, and he has been our abbot for twenty years." "Brother," said that abbot sternly, "do not jest with me. Open the gate now, and let me in." And then he noticed that the monk's face was becoming white with fear. "Abbot John!" the monk gasped. "We have had no Abbot John here for three hundred years. The last Abbot John was sometime around 1400. It is now 1704!"

The reverse of this story is related, I believe, about the Prophet Mohammed, who is said to have been rapt into heaven for seven long years in the interval between letting a pitcher of water slip from his hand and catching it again before it could spill. . . . In fact there is a universal tradition about moments in which people have slipped out of time into eternity—and very often come back into time at the most unexpected and inconvenient places! These stories are not always of a religious character. It is said that when even the fastest pitcher sent a ball to Babe Ruth, the moment of striking it was slowed down in his mind to such a point that he could see the seams on the ball with perfect clarity. There was once, too, an experimenter with dreams who ran an icicle across the neck of a sleeping man, who then woke to relate a long, long dream about his adventures in the French Revolution that ended up with his being guillotined.

By and large, however, this universal tradition of the eternal moment is especially associated with spiritual experience and with the arts—and always it carries the implication that there is some very special and splendid insight to be discovered in a kind of concentration upon the immediate moment. It is as if one were to find out that the moment in which we live is a sort of keyhole through which one may pass into a world in which—on the one hand—time does not rush by and—on the other hand—life is not merely dead and static. It is to discover that the whole point of being alive does not lie in some future destination, some far-off ideal yet to be attained, but that in some very queer way, this particular instant in which we are living is the fulfillment of everything and leaves nothing more that is of any real importance to be desired.

You might naturally imagine that a person who could feel this way would thereupon be good for nothing else. They would be deprived of incentive to create or achieve anything. They would loaf idly through the rest of their days, enraptured with nothing but the contemplation of their immediate present. I realize that this is what would *seem* to happen, but I know equally well that it is not the case, though I do not know why it is not. This may be paradox or nonsense, but the truth is that those who have ever discovered the complete sufficiency of this one moment become extraordinarily creative people. As a matter of fact, some approximation to this point of view is the only state of mind in which we can cope with some of the most difficult kinds of work—work that appears endless, boring, and insuperably frustrating. We have to take each step as if it were the only one to be taken—and then the job is done before we know it.

Once upon a time there was a judge who complained to a Buddhist priest that his work—trying one silly case after another—was an intolerable bore, and he asked the priest what could he do about it. The priest wrote him the following poem:

Not twice this day:
Inch, time, foot, gem.

After such a vivid expression it is perhaps anticlimactic to add that he was saying that every single inch and foot of time is a unique gem. Ordinarily this does not seem to be so, because we have formed the habit of comparing each moment with past and future moments, and of adding the moments together in our minds so that they present an appalling monotony. The unique gem cannot be found unless we live each moment without comparing it with others, and without adding it to others, treating it as if it were the only one to be lived.

But this seems to be neither easy nor practical. It might seem to require a state of amnesia, the difficult and probably dangerous step of wiping all other moments out of memory and thus losing the thread of coherence and purpose in our lives. This would be true if it were impossible for us to live, as it were, on two levels at once; but in fact it is not at all impossible, since we are doing it constantly. I pointed out a little while ago that while from a relative standpoint we are certainly moving through space, from an absolute standpoint we are neither moving nor still, going through time neither swiftly nor slowly. This is living on two levels at once.

From a relative standpoint, from within the framework of certain conventions and social institutions, our lives have purpose and meaning. But there is another standpoint from which we are not going anywhere but nowhere, from which all the complex and marvelous creations of human culture are like the intricate but meaningless patterns of bubbles on the seashore. For sanity's sake we need to see both viewpoints. We need to be able to live with the future clearly in mind; but we need also to be able to see the total perfection of every instant. These points are not mutually exclusive. I cannot explain *why* they are not, because all language is geared to the realm of relativity and can only conceive what is more perfect by comparison with what is less perfect. So to understand this, you have to go beyond words, to realize that even quite ordinary experiences cannot really be described with words, and that there is a great deal more to life than what we can think about in verbal symbols.

I said a moment ago that the experience of the eternal moment is a kind of concentration upon this particular instant, as if it were the only one to be lived. That "kind of" is important, because it is not concentration as usually understood, as a fixed staring. If you stare fixedly at this moment, trying to get something out of it, it will elude you on the spot. It will be like trying to chop a ball bearing with a hatchet. When you think very hard about this moment, you can't put your finger on it, you can't find it. It is just a fleeting infinitesimal, that is never here at all. It is always just about to be and always just gone by.

Concentration in the sense in which I am using the word means, not staring at, but being centered in this one moment and not comparing it with any other. It requires simply the understanding that there *is* no other moment than this one: there never was, and there never will be. It moves faster than lightning, and yet—in a kind of Alice-Through-the-Looking-Glass fashion—it is always here. It changes with the insta-bility of smoke, and yet is ever the same. You cannot, then, compare this moment with any other, for there are no oth-ers. Memories of the past and anticipation of the future are not other moments, but parts of this one. When you try to compare them with it, you are trying to compare this moment with itself—and nothing is more frustrating than trying to do the impossible.

The thought that there is just this moment, and no other one, is at first sight against all common sense. It seems so completely obvious that there most certainly will be other moments, that tomorrow will soon be here, with the very concrete reality of its work to be done and its pains and travails to be suffered. True. But if you look at the matter clearly, it becomes suddenly quite obvious that you cannot experience any other moment than this one with any degree of vivid reality. Think of the very worst that could happen tomorrow. Feel free to worry about it just as much as you like. But actually, in vivid reality, there is nothing in the world except just this worrying. Well then—why not worry? Why not give yourself up, with all the energy at your command, to a real orgy of anxiety? Since there is nothing else at the moment, one may as well make the best of it. But . . . let me ask you, what sort of an experience does anxiety become when you are so immersed in it that you have nothing else to compare it with? This is the same problem as how long is a piece of string. It is the same as asking whether a snail is going slowly when *not* being compared with an airplane or the hour hand of a clock.

One cannot live this moment completely, without comparison, so long as it still seems that there might be some other real alternative. But one has to find out, first of all, that there is actually nothing else to do. And there isn't. Everything else is a straining after shadows and clutching at winds; and if one *must* strain after shadows, well go ahead and strain. There is a saying in Zen Buddhism, "Walk or sit just as you will, but whatever you do, don't wobble"—to which I would add, but if you *must* wobble, wobble with all your might. "The fool who persists in their folly will become wise." But they must persist with the whole energy of their soul.

Perhaps we can now begin to see it has been said that all the riches that the heart could desire, why the ultimate mystery of the universe, or whatever you want to call it, is not to be found far away in some distant place in a remote future. The universal tradition of the timeless moment insists that it is all right here, and that if you cannot find it in this immediate instant, you cannot find it at all, because there is no other place to look. But no one in the world can explain why it should be so, or can convince you by argument that it is worth looking into. It is so much easier to try it for oneself, and see into the thing directly. Let me conclude with two more Zen poems, which say it so much better than I can. There is one about "idle thoughts," which means comparisons between one moment and another.

> In spring, hundreds of flowers;
> In summer, the breeze;
> In autumn, the falling leaves;
> In winter, snow.
> Free your mind from idle thoughts,
> And every season is a good season.

And in case this sounds too much like a rural rhapsody, there is this other:

> Under the sword lifted high
> Is hell, making you tremble.
> But go straight ahead,
> And there is the Land of Bliss.

2. The Illusion of Time

It was probably harder to realize a thousand years ago. Today it seems to me that no reflective person can possibly fail to see it. Somewhere in the makeup of the human mind as we know it there is a mistake—a radical and possibly fatal error. I don't think any reasonable person can expose themself to the media of mass communication in our world—the press, the radio, the TV—not to mention the dangerous networks of automotive transportation, without beginning to realize that we are the victims of a collective insanity. On the surface it seems to be a highly complex disease arising from innumerable causes, all of them so deeply involved and ingrained that nothing can be done about it. But I can't escape the insistent intuition that it is not quite that way—that the causes are not numerous, that they do not lie beyond recall in an inaccessible past, nor buried in deep-seated and intractable patterns of blind emotion. I feel that there is something difficult, but not at all impossible, to understand because it is so close to us that it escapes notice—a sort of unconscious, unexamined assumption about life that might be corrected relatively easily if only it could be brought to light.

This could be wishful thinking. On the other hand, people who are accustomed to philosophical, mathematical, or scientific thought soon discover that when their thinking begins to contradict itself absurdly and to move in inextricably complicated vicious circles, there is probably something wrong with the premises. There was usually a simple mistake at the very beginning, which throws everything out of order. The subsequent calculations may have been made accurately and cleverly, but the initial mistake undermines them so irretrievably that no amount of skill can produce order if one continues to follow the same line. There is nothing for it but to go back to the beginning.

In human affairs, however, it seems that this is the one thing that we cannot possibly do. For we believe that our present state of affairs is the consequence of a long course of history. And history takes place in a one-way stream of time in which there is no going back to beginnings. If there were a mistake in the beginning, we are stuck with it. On rare occasions, a single individual may perhaps free themself from some of the consequences of their past. But as we move from the individual to the collective, actions become more and more determined, and we move into a realm where the present is almost wholly dictated by the past and the past remains fixed beyond recall. We know, for example, that it is very difficult to predict events in the submicroscopic world, to predict the so-called Brownian movements of very minute particles. But when such movements are considered in the mass, collectively, prediction becomes much easier, and a determinism seems more and more firmly established. It is perhaps the same with individuals on the one hand and societies on the other.

Yet somehow I suspect that the radical error of which I was speaking is closely connected with this very view of history. For I feel that our collective insanity has something to do with our sensation, or our idea, of time. Time has always fascinated me. I don't mean time in the sense of rhythm or tempo. I mean continuous time, which is always getting later and later, the ineluctable life-movement from the past into the future. It's so inescapably real, and yet so strangely intangible and indefinable. But I cannot get over the enormous hunch that there's something wrong with it—that somewhere in our commonsense view of time there is a radical illusion.

There are, I believe, some good and fairly obvious reasons for thinking that the root of the difficulty has something to do with time. For it is often said that the basic instinct of living organisms is for survival, which means of going on in time. The need to survive involves struggle, conflict, anxiety. Furthermore, in our technological civilization time seems much more real and much more important than in simpler cultures. Our satisfactions are more than ever projected into the future. Tomorrow assumes an ever-growing significance— to the degree that happiness eludes us in the present. To say that something has no future is to damn it outright. On the other hand, to *have* a future is the measure of value, and this future is what we pursue at ever-increasing speeds.

Here on the West Coast of America we can see this in a peculiarly vivid way, for we are all on wheels rather than legs. We move incessantly, and often to no other purpose than to be somewhere else. Vast networks of superhighways and air-lines are making it easier and easier to travel to places that are less and less worth visiting because they are more and more alike. Industry creates a growing multitude of utterly indistinguishable towns. I don't need to underline the conformist spirit of American, Russian, and all industrialized life. The maddening monotony grows upon us not only in space and shape, but also in time—in a succession of days that tend to be more and more alike as we move away from the old culture of festivals and fasts that gave the year a definite design. We are now too busy to feast and too greedy to fast, and thus the time, the future time, into which we are racing promises to be increasingly monotonous. And we wonder why adventurous children start smashing things and why sensitive adults get

roaring drunk or retreat into the relatively fascinating fanta-
sies of psychosis.

It is in vain that the moralists and the preachers call for
restraint, sacrifice, and abstinence from desire; nevertheless,
there is something right in what they are saying. The notion
that human sanity has a good deal to do with self-restraint
has persisted for many thousands of years and has had some
very wise exponents. But it has usually had an end in view—a
temporal, future end—some sort of pie in the sky. No one can
really abstain, however, no one can effectively overcome the
mad greed of anxiety, until they have realized that the future
is a mirage that does not contain the answer to anything. The
true ascetic is not forcing themself; they are just acting naturally in accordance with reality as they see it. I think it was
Father Huntington, founder of the Anglican Order of the Holy
Cross, who made the remarkable statement that spiritual perfection consists in walking slowly. Yet this is not a matter of
"hold your horses," of patience as a fierce tension with the for-
ward rush of time and desire. The problem is simpler in that
it needs less energy, but more difficult in that it is not at all
obvious. What is required is not brilliant brains, but a kind of
revolutionary simplicity.

Perhaps it sounds fantastic to say that the really urgent
thing is not to put a stop to war and atom bombs and totalitarian governments, but to put a stop to time. Words confuse
us, and time means too many things. Let me say again, I do
not mean time in the special senses of rhythm and growth.
I mean the entirely monotonous, rhythmless, continuously

accelerating time, the time in which things do not grow but merely move, the time wherein, indeed, things are not given time to grow but must be forced into fruition faster and faster. It is not really fantastic to talk about stopping this kind of time; it is one of the few processes we can stop—for the simple reason that it is not real.

I don't think it is enough to see that this kind of time is not going anywhere, for this insight seldom gives us much more than fits of depression. Vanity of vanities, all flesh is as the grass, the caravan starting for the dawn of Nothing—all that is not quite the point. It is only part of the problem, albeit an important part, to see that, in the not so very long run, we *have* no future. This is the negative aspect of the insight that we need. But there is also a positive aspect, an aspect that more than makes up for the depressing deprivation of the thought that the dimension of time leads only to annihilation, or to what may be worse, infinite monotony—which used to be called everlasting damnation.

The traditional opposite of everlasting damnation was called eternal—that is, timeless—life, and however much vagueness may have surrounded it, there has been general agreement that it was in some way peculiarly wonderful and splendid. It never really had very much to do with halos, harps, and hymns for always and always; this was only a rather crude symbolism for something so much easier to understand that ordinary language was too complicated to express it. If I may continue with the use of this traditional language for a while, I think we should try to grasp what was really meant by the difference between time and eternity, between earth and heaven, the natural and the supernatural, the relative and the absolute.

Perhaps I can best show the difference between the two by an illustration from music. When we listen to a melody, or just a changing succession of notes, we think of these notes as high or low, long or short. It is obvious, however, that the individual notes are not high or low, long or short, in themselves, but in relation to each other. This comparison, and the consequent recognition of a melody, is made possible because we can retain in memory notes that are no longer being sounded—notes that are in some sense no longer real. And in this sense of the word, the real note, that which is being sounded right now, is not in itself high or low, long or short. The same is true of the series or succession of thoughts or events that we call life. The distinctions of good and bad, pleasant and painful, fast and slow, are relative—and depend upon retaining the past in memory. For purposes of this illustration, the notes or events as compared with one another will stand for the relative world. On the other hand, the present note or event, considered by itself, will stand for the absolute world, since in itself, the note is timeless. You will remember, too, that traditional descriptions of the absolute world are apt to be composed mostly of denials of its relativity. It is called that which is neither good nor bad, high nor low, long nor short, existing nor non-existing. And yet it is also called the one and only reality, just as the note that is sounded now is, in a sense, the only real one.

At this point, I am sure it does not sound as if the so-called absolute world is very exciting. For the whole significance of a melody depends on the mutual relations of the notes. If we were somehow to forget these relations, surely the notes would all seem to be the same. Well, certainly not—because the sense of sameness depends upon comparison just as much as the sense of difference. Be that as it may, it would nevertheless seem that a mind in which passing events left no more trace than the passage of birds through the sky, a mind in which there was no comparison between events, would be in a subhuman state of idiocy without any conscious intelligence at all. This would doubtless be true if it were also true that the two worlds—the relative and the absolute—were mutually exclusive, if hearing a note by itself made it impossible to hear it in relation to other notes. But this is not how it works.

Disentangling the mind from the illusion of time requires primarily an act of concentration that is perhaps best made in the form of a question. I want to know what is really happening, what I am actually and certainly experiencing, and not just imagining or remembering. One does not handle this question by trying to think it out, but by feeling or sensing, to see what is actually there. Only in asking this question one must by very careful not to strain and stare, as if concentration required a muscular effort. This will only put the mind in a kind of cramp. If you want to see something clearly, there are two extremes to be avoided—staring at it until you eyes water, fuzzing the image, or looking so loosely that your eyes go out of focus. So then—with eyes and ears, senses and feelings all resting in focus, we look directly at whatever happens to be here. Without any very great difficulty we should, I think, be able to see that in plain fact the only thing we see is what I have called the absolute world—a now without past or future.

Now all this is very much like playing with an optical illusion. At first glance it seems perfectly obvious that in this drawing of three men in a passage, the three are of different sizes. But look again, and it is clear that they are all the same size. Yet the impression, created by the perspective lines of the passage, that the man at the back is ever so much taller than the man in front keeps returning, and only after continued readjustment of the mind does it become obvious, even at a glance, that their sizes are equal. It is the same with the psychological illusion of time. It has the tremendous persuasive force of long habit, and although seeing through it is not really difficult, the mind so easily slips back into its old rut. Yet it can adjust itself to the new standpoint, and then it becomes just as self-evident, just as much a matter of common sense, that the real world is actually timeless. The illusion of time and of relativity can still be seen, but seen *as* an illusion, bereft of its persuasive power. What now appears as the fundamental and primary reality is not a series of events, relatively good and bad, long and short; the fundamental reality is just *this* event—sufficient in itself without yesterday or tomorrow. What has happened is not that the absolute view has destroyed the relative, but that the emphasis of reality has shifted in such a way that the reality of the timeless world is far more persuasive than that of the world of time.

The correction of this basic illusion naturally brings about a large number of psychological changes, and one of the most interesting is the disappearance of the sense of rush, of temporal urgency and anxiety. You begin to realize how your whole consciousness has been cramped and stifled by rush, how the moments have whizzed by without yielding any real satisfaction, for paradoxical as it may sound, to take time seriously is to have no time! Habituated as we are to the panic of time-consciousness, we are even persuaded that there is something wise and good about it, and fear that without the sense of rush human beings would lose all incentive and creative interest.

Now this is the most fantastic nonsense. Human beings are, I think, the only creatures who rush. Plants and animals create themselves in the most wonderful variety of forms, but they never hurry. All their processes of growth depend upon the most admirable timing, for, as I said before, rush is the polar opposite of real time, which is growth and rhythm. Rush is likewise completely inimical to human creativeness: artists, inventors, and writers cannot work properly when they are rushed, because speed gives their thoughts no time to grow and mature. This is why our current culture produces such a terrifying amount of sloppy workmanship in everything from clothing and housing to so-called works of art. It is all slammed together without love or patience, in a huge hurry to make money for things that aren't worth buying.

We pretend that we cannot afford real craftsmen. They are already an almost obsolete race. We argue that they were after all a luxury for a leisured aristocracy, as if the only alternative to a leisured aristocracy were a harried mob of bourgeois-proletarians owning immense quantities of rubbish.

I feel it is a very healthy sign of some remnants of sanity that more and more people are ceasing to buy certain kinds of trash and are spending their leisure hours making some of the essentials of life for themselves—houses, furniture, dishes, clothing—and there are signs that this is beginning to go far beyond a mere hobby. I am acquainted, too, with more and more young people who show not the least enthusiasm for the sundry squirrel cages of business and industry, and who would much rather live in poverty doing work that is sincere and true to their sense of vocation. But in some respects these are simply the symptoms of unbearable discomfort. They do not yet go to what seems to me to be the root of the matter, to that basic slip of the mind's eye into the optical illusion of the kind of time whose symbol is the monotonous, rhythm-less, uniform motion of the clock . . . that silly gadget that attempts to count our hours and whereby we persuade ourselves that they are really and truly numbered, that attempts to divide life into equal units and measures—hours, days, months, and years—which never actually fit in with the essentially non-mechanical rhythms of growth and of the seasons and of the earth's rotation about the sun.

If anyone wants to join a *real* revolution, something far beyond changing from the right side to the left on the hard bed of politics, beyond the ideological isms that are merely symptoms battling with symptoms—I suggest that for a real revolution we start a new leisured aristocracy, not of privilege and material wealth, but of people who won't rush or be rushed, out of the clear realization that clock-measured time is an illusion. I cannot feel that there is really very much to lose by this, except in mere quantity. We shall exchange all that money for what little we have, a bird in the hand being worth two in the bush. And far, far more important than this, we shall exchange the purely imaginary and utterly frustrating fantasy of the numbered days hurrying by for the actual reality of this one unique event—neither long nor short, neither fast nor slow, but eternal.

3. Christianity and Nature

The original meaning of the word "pagan" is country-dweller, and the word came to be identified with "heathen" because the first Christian communities grew up in the cities. I do not think that nearly enough weight has been given to this fact. The urban origins of Christianity may have a great deal to do with something that has puzzled me all my life, and I can only express this puzzle in a rather personal way.

To put it briefly: I can only feel like a Christian when I am indoors; I am incapable of being one in the open air. I have a very deep love and respect for the rites and doctrines of the Catholic Church. For me, the whole culture of European Catholicism—something very different from American Catholicism—is one of the most marvelous and beautiful things on earth. I love and respect not only its outward and aesthetic aspect, but also its inward center—the spirit of sanctity that has animated the lives of the Christian saints. But I can maintain this love and respect only by keeping it in a water-tight compartment, by shutting out the light of the open sky with the symbolic jewelry of stained-glass windows.

I feel that there is a deep and quite extraordinary incompatibility between the beauty of Christianity and the beauty of nature. Speaking personally still, I have always found it quite impossible to relate God the Father, Jesus Christ, the angels, and the saints to the universe in which I actually live. The moment I see a tree or look into a flower, or glance at the sky and the stars, or look at a naked human body, or go down to the ocean to watch the waves, I find myself in a world where this religion simply does not fit. The inconsistency is not so much intellectual as aesthetic, for what I feel is an incompatibility of character, of style. No one, for example, would dream of attributing a landscape by Sesshu to Constable or Cézanne, or a symphony by Haydn to Schoenberg or Palestrina. In the same way, my feeling for the style of Christianity, whether Catholic or Protestant, makes it completely impossible for me to identify the author of this religion with the author of the physical universe. This is not a judgment as to the relative merits of the two styles; it is only to say that they are not by the same hand and that they do not mix well together.

Now I could well imagine a theologian who might say to me, "This is very understandable. For the beauty of the physical world is natural, and the beauty of Christianity is supernatural. The nearest thing in the physical world to supernatural beauty is the beauty of the human being, and more especially of the human mind. This is why you connect Christianity with the urban rather than the rural atmosphere, because in the urban atmosphere you are surrounded by the works of humanity."

"It is true," they might go on to say, "that in a rural environment you are surrounded by the works of God. But humanity, and even the creations of humanity, are far higher works of God than anything you can find elsewhere in nature. Thus they reveal more of the character of God than the sun, moon, and stars, the clouds and the waters, for what we sometimes call the artificial is nearer to the supernatural than the natural."

And then they might add: "In what you have said so far, I think I can detect a slight prejudice in favor of the beauty of nature—and that is because you are a sentimentalist. You love the aesthetic surfaces of nature, so long as you do not have to struggle for life, which underlies it. It is only in humanity that there have arisen ethical and moral ideas that, as it were, give nature a feeling heart—and this, again, goes to show that you will not find God reflected anywhere in nature so clearly as in humanity. Now it is true," they would say, "that we often want to seek relief from the hideousness of crowds and cities in the solitude of nature, but this is only because the worst is the corruption of the best. The evil of humanity is far more terrible than the evil of the serpent or the shark, but only because the goodness of humanity immeasurably exceeds the goodness of a spring landscape. You have only to consider how utterly lonely and lost you would feel if you were the only human being in the world. How glad you would then be to exchange the whole sum of natural beauty for a single human face."

This begins to sound like a convincing argument until you realize that it contains a very curious premise, implied in the idea that I might be willing to exchange the whole sum of natural beauty for a single human face. This is not an exchange, for the beauty of humanity is, inseparably, part of the total sum of natural beauty. Furthermore, the discrepancy of style that I feel between Christianity and nature includes, within nature, the human form—especially when it is not the pale and potatoish thing grown in cities under the influence of ill-conceived clothing and sedentary living. I often wonder whether the hatred of Caucasians for the other races is not a concealed form of envy.

To some of you, this line of thought may be beginning to sound like something that, in sophisticated circles, is now regarded as a rather comic romanticism. I am thinking of the back-to-nature fads: nudism, vegetarianism, the cult of the soil, homespun clothing, beachcombing in the South Seas, and all that. In modern times this kind of thing has been a reaction against both Christianity and industrialism, and for all that may be fanatical, comic, utopian, and faddist in movements of this type, I do not think we can seriously deny that they have a point, that there is really something to be said for a certain amount of neo-paganism.

This becomes rather easier to see when we compare our own culture, not with those of the South Sea Islands, but with the highly sophisticated and even urbanized cultures of the Far East, of China and Japan. For here we simply do not find this peculiar discrepancy between religion and nature—at least, not to anything like the extent as with Christianity. It is particularly significant that the really great Buddhist art of both China and Japan is landscape painting, and that both the Buddhist and the Taoist conception of the perfect temple is not the stone church that shuts nature out but the wooden roof with sliding walls that lets nature in. One of the rather fascinating symptoms of the compatibility of Buddhism and the incompatibility of Christianity with the natural universe is that it is practically impossible to represent the crucifixion in the Chinese style of painting! I have seen it tried, and the results are extremely weird. The reason is simply that the symmetrical form of the cross completely destroys the rhythm of a Chinese painting if it is permitted to be the principal image in the picture. Chinese Christians have tried to solve the problem by painting rustic crosses with bark and moss still on the wood, and stumps of branches protruding from the main beams. But these two straight seams simply jar with the rest of the painting, and the artist cannot follow their natural tendency to bend the straight lines irregularly without destroying the symbol of the cross.

This in itself is perhaps a rather trivial example, but it serves as a parable, an illustration that will show us something of the essential difference between pagan and Christian beauty. The reason the form of the cross is so foreign to Chinese painting is that the Chinese artist follows nature in loving forms that are flowing, jagged, and asymmetrical—forms eminently suited to their media, the brush and black ink. When, on the other hand, we consider the art forms of Christianity, the Byzantine and Gothic, we find a love of the architectural and the courtly. For God is conceived in the image of a throned monarch, and the rituals of the Church are patterned after the court ceremonials of the Greco-Roman emperors. Likewise in the ancient Hebrew religion, the Ark of the Covenant was essentially a throne hidden in the inner sanctuary of the Holy of Holies, which was built in the form of a perfect cube, since the cube was considered the symbol of completeness and perfection.

Yet from the standpoint of Chinese philosophy and aesthetics, this symmetrical and architectonic perfection is rigid and lifeless. Such forms are found but rarely in nature. So, too, the Chinese conceived of the power behind nature not in the image of a monarch but as the Tao, the course or flow, and found images for it in water and wind, in the air and the sky, as well as in the processes of growth. Furthermore, there was no sense that the Tao had any desire to obtrude itself or to shine like a monarch. For the Tao is always anonymous and unknown, and the incessant changefulness and impermanence of nature are used as a symbol of the fact that the Tao can never be grasped or conceived in any fixed form.

Furthermore, the Chinese have realized a distinction between the natural and the artificial that seems to have escaped the Western mind almost entirely. This is the truth that natural forms are not made, but grown—that there is a radical difference between the organic and the mechanical. Things that are made—such as houses, furniture, and machines—are an assemblage of parts put together, or shaped, like sculpture, from the outside inward. But things that grow shape themselves from within outward; they are not an assemblage of originally distinct parts: they partition themselves, elaborating their own structure from the whole to the parts, from the simple to the complex.

This is why it is impossible for one who sees this difference to think of the natural universe as something made. It is just here, I feel, that we have the key to the total difference of style between the forms of Christianity and the forms of nature. In the Church, we are in a universe that has been made. Outside the Church, we are in a universe that has grown. Thus the God who made the world stands outside it as the carpenter stands outside their table, whereas the Tao that grows the world is within it. Christian theology admits, in theory, that God is immanent, within all things. But only in theory. In practice it is God's transcendence, God's outsideness, that is emphasized, and furthermore, God is only permitted to dwell on the inside on the strict condition that he maintains an immense qualitative difference between himself and the creature that he inhabits. Even on the inside God is outside, as the architect is still really outside the house that they build, even when they go in to decorate the interior.

This leads us to a further distinction of the greatest importance between the Western and the Chinese conceptions of nature and of God. Conceiving humanity and the universe as made, the Western and Christian mind endeavors to interpret them mechanically. The Christian Westerner has an *idée fixe* that the universe consists of distinct things or entities, which are like mechanical parts. They feel strange to this natural environment, thinking of their soul as something that has come into it from the outside, as a part is introduced into a house or a machine. Furthermore, they try to understand the workings of the natural universe in terms of logical laws—laws that may be expressed in streamlined, mathematical forms of a regular and symmetrical character. They measure the earth and the skies by approximating the wayward and whimsical shapes of nature to the circles, triangles, and straight lines of Mr. Euclid. If they come actually to believe that nature *is* a mechanism, this is because they can only grasp as much of nature as they can fit into some mechanical or mathematical analogy. As a result, they never really see nature. All they really see is the pattern of geometrical forms that they have managed to project upon it.

It is thus one of the strangest paradoxes that whereas Christianity insists so strongly that God is personal and living, the nature of God as conceived in practice has all the attributes of personality except the most central and important— which is why it is so terribly difficult to love God except as a discipline. For God is really conceived as a set of principles— principles of morality, of justice, of reason, of science, and of

art. Even his love is principled, since it is tempered with justice, with the qualities of Eros. Absent from this conception is,
as I said, the most essential element of any living personality,
the element that I will call inwardness.

What is inwardness? As I just pointed out, living things,
organisms, grow from within outward. They do not fashion
themselves by standing outside themselves like architects
or mechanics. (And, incidentally, when human beings try to
develop themselves in this way, the results are always affected,
artificial, and insincere.) But the very nature of inwardness is
to be mysterious, immeasurable, and unpredictable. For what
is truly inward can never become an object. It is because of the
inwardness of our life process that we do not know, or rather,
cannot tell how or why we live—even though it is our inmost
selves that are doing the living. The difficulty with God, as
conceived in Christianity, is that he knows himself through
and through; he knows everything—and for this reason lacks
an inside. He is fashioned in the image of Western man as
he would like himself to be—a being in total control of himself, analyzed to the ultimate depths of his own unconscious,
understood and explained to the last atom of his brain, and to
this extent completely mechanized. When every last element
of inwardness has become an object of knowledge, the being
is reduced to nothing but a rattling shell.

Thus when I leave the Church and the city behind, and go
out under the great sky; when I am with the birds, for all their
voraciousness, and with the clouds for all their thunders, and
the oceans for all their tempests and submerged monsters, I

cannot feel in a Christian way because I am in a world that grows from within. I am simply incapable of feeling its life as coming from above, from beyond the stars, even recognizing that this is a figure of speech. To put it more exactly, I cannot feel that its life comes from Another, from someone who is other than, who is qualitatively and spiritually external to, all that lives and grows. On the contrary, I feel this whole world to be moved from the inside, and from an inside so deep that its inside is my inside too. I feel the most peculiar kinship with it, since it is a kinship that relates not only to what is sympathetic and obviously beautiful. I feel kin even to what strikes me as horrendous and strange, because I know that there are also seemingly monstrous shapes and inhuman processes within my own body.

Long before Easter celebrated the resurrection of Christ, it was the pagan feast of growth, of the natural miracle of birth out of the unconscious and inward, rather than the "technological" miracle of the corpse brought back to life and the stone rolled away from the tomb. To me, it is an incomparably greater miracle—even though it happens many times a day—that a child is born, than that once a dead man came back to life. For in this latter miracle there is something unnatural because unnecessary or irrelevant. The raising of the dead—when you mean by this the revivification of a corpse—can appear as a real marvel only to those who feel that death is apart from life, who feel it is a return to the inward, to the unknown from which I came when I was born. I do not mean this literally, because there is no biological resemblance between death and birth. Death is not simply reversed birth. I mean, rather, that the truly inward source of my life was never born, that it has always remained inside, in somewhat the same way as the life remains in the tree, though the fruits may come and go. Outwardly, I am one apple among many. Inwardly, I am the tree.

Perhaps this was what Christ really meant when he said, "I am the Vine; you are the branches." Christianity is by no means *necessarily* the unnatural thing I have described, for there are hints within its rich mythology that that mechanical-looking, rigid cross is really a tree. I am thinking of the ancient hymn that says:

> Faithful Cross above all other,
> One and only noble Tree;
> None in foliage, none in blossom,
> None in fruit thy peer may be.
> Sweetest wood and sweetest iron,
> Sweetest weight is hung on thee.

There is also, within the Christian tradition, the old and universal myth of the blossoming staff—the famous Rod of Jesse. This is, of course, what must happen if the Chinese artist is to be able to paint the crucifixion of Christ. The rigid cross of dead wood must blossom, and turn into a living tree. This would, indeed, be a marvelous fulfillment or fruition of the Christian story. For there is a legend that the wood of the cross upon which Christ was crucified was taken from that Tree of Knowledge in the Garden of Eden, the eating of whose fatal fruit brought about the Fall of Adam, so that he was expelled from Eden and debarred from eating the fruit of the other tree that stood there—the Tree of Life. Now the kind of knowledge that involves the Fall of Man is precisely that of which I have been speaking: the knowledge of nature that turns it into a mechanism, that tries to turn all inwardness into outwardness, seeking fruit only to find husks. This is the cross upon which the Christ suffers, if Christ stands for the inward life that is in us all. And the crucifixion still remains in vain if it does not bring about the transformation of the Tree of Knowledge and Death into the Tree of Life. This is why the ancient hymn that I have just quoted continues:

> Bend thy boughs, O Tree of Glory,
> Thy relaxing sinews bend.
> For a while the ancient rigor
> Which thy birth bestowed, suspend;
> And the King of heavenly beauty
> On thy bosom gently tend.

But this is what has not yet happened. The old rugged cross remains, and the prayer of this hymn will not be answered until the day when the Christian cross bends its boughs, relaxes its sinews, and becomes at last the Tree of Life.

4. A Cure for Education

When children begin to study arithmetic, they learn that two and two are absolutely and necessarily four. This is drummed into them with the weight of authority, since children are capricious creatures and, if left to themselves, will discover all sorts of wayward answers for two plus two. But if—as is seldom the case—the child ever gets to the point where they can go rather more deeply into the mysteries of mathematics, they may discover, with some degree of concentration, that this absolute law of two plus two "ain't necessarily so." It depends on what kinds of things you are adding. Indeed, if they go still further, they find that nothing is absolutely so at all. They will discover whole systems of mathematics based on premises that seem to be completely absurd—as, for example, that four axes at right angles to one another can intersect at one point, giving us the mathematics of four dimensions, or, for that matter, as many dimensions as you like.

But this isn't going to be a talk about mathematics. I have mentioned these things as instances of the whole problem of unlearning, or, shall I say, of correcting necessary and unavoidable mistakes. To put it briefly, what we call upbringing or education is a way of making children conform to the conventions of society. This seems to be entirely necessary. But in the process, most children are—perhaps unavoidably—warped. They lose their innocence, their spontaneity, their unselfconsciousness. In psychological jargon, they develop all kinds of inner conflicts and complexes, and they do not seem to be able to recover from them in adult life without the expensive luxury of psychoanalysis or some similar kind of therapy. And even then, I am not quite sure how often they really recover.

If you persevere in the science of mathematics, you will eventually find out that the absolute rules that you learned in the beginning were strictly conventional, and were not in any sense fixed laws of nature. But you can complete four years of college, become a parent, and reach the top of your business or profession, without ever "seeing through" the absolutes of conduct and feeling, of thinking and reasoning, that were so firmly implanted in you as a child. To put it in another way, you can go through the whole of life without ever getting out of the splints and crutches, the spectacles and hearing aids, that were used to train your mind in the beginning. The result is that conventional disciplines do not become the mere instruments of free minds; they become the very structure of the mind itself, so that for all our boasting about living in the "land of the free," we are no more free than Dr. Pavlov's dogs.

This may be the inevitable price of civilization and culture. What you gain upon the roundabout, you lose upon the swings, or, as Ogden Nash put it:

The trouble with a kitten is THAT
Eventually it becomes a CAT

It may be that the refreshing naturalness of the child is something that the civilized adult loses as irreplaceably as the cat its kittenishness. But I do not think this is a proper analogy. I have lived a lot with cats, and I much prefer them to kittens. Furthermore, I have from time to time met with adults—highly sophisticated and cultured adults—who have somehow regained, or perhaps never lost, their unaffected spontaneity. It does not seem to me to be a necessary law that an advanced culture requires the loss of these natural qualities.

I am not trying in any way to idealize the child. With five of them, I know better than that! The point is that children begin to develop certain virtues that, as a result of their upbringing, they do not continue to develop. Social conventions require them to develop their orderliness and skill rather than their simplicity and unaffectedness, since the two types of virtue seem to be mutually exclusive at a young age. If this is the cost of civilization, there is a serious question as to whether the cost is not much too great, as to whether—indeed—it may not eventually be fatal to civilization.

Perhaps I can try to define, or at least to suggest, the qualities that we are losing. These are qualities that the child exhibits in a rather primitive and embryonic form, and which one finds more fully developed only in the most exceptional people. To use psychological jargon again, we say that people of this rare type are integrated. That's to say, they are not at cross-purposes with themselves; they do not get in their own way and stand in their own light. They are what the Gospels call "single-eyed," for "if thine eye be single, thy whole body shall be full of light." We call this trait sincerity—the virtue of not being self-deceived, of not thinking one thing and feeling another, or of not feeling one thing and trying to feel another.

It is, furthermore, the marvelous quality of unselfconsciousness—the quality of the person who can think, act, and live
without anxious side-glances at themselves that spoil the
directness and effectiveness of their action. And this lack of
self-consciousness involves something else besides, of a still
deeper order. A truly unselfconscious person feels related
to their environment, or rather, integrated with their environment. To put it in another way, they do not experience
any gulf or gap between their own inner workings—their
thoughts and feelings—and the natural processes going on
around them. And thus they have a kind of unaggressive but
nonetheless unshakable assurance, which at a deep level is
religious faith, or at its deepest level a kind of metaphysical
certainty. I do not mean by this that one is certain as to the
truth of some idea or proposition. What I call a metaphysical
certainty cannot really be put into words at all, for it is more
nearly a feeling, shall I say a feeling of the inescapable naturalness and rightness of everything that one feels and does, even
when it is perfectly clear that, from a relative standpoint, one
is in the wrong.

Most civilized adults, and especially those who belong to
the Anglo-Saxon cultures of the West, do not have this kind
of naturalness, nor the unmistakable kind of gaiety that
goes with it. They seem to carry themselves heavily—to be
so haunted by self-awareness that even when they feel themselves to be 100 percent sincere and in the right, they must
needs insist upon it—as if there might be some doubt about
it. For when the process of the cultural conditioning has not

been unlearned, the human mind gets stuck in a perpetual self-criticism, a perpetual division against itself, which in the end paralyzes creative action.

There are some who feel that children can be brought up without warping them, that with loving and skillful care they may be taught the conventions and artificialities of society without losing their naturalness. If this is true, I am sure that it can only be done by the very rare kind of adult I have been talking about. Therefore this doesn't seem to be a very practical answer to the problem.

Yet the problem has been solved—to some degree at least—in other cultures: cultures that have what might be called regular institutions for curing people of their upbringing, or of the inevitable distortions that it involves. It is like salting meat to preserve it, and then soaking out the excess salt before putting it on the table to be eaten.

There are some rather interesting historical reasons why we do not have this kind of cultural institution. The most important is that we have identified our social and moral conventions with the will of God, with the Absolute itself. That is to say, we have weighted them with altogether excessive authority. As a result, a person who feels a conflict between a moral convention and their natural feelings finds themself at odds, not only with their family or their community, but with the very root and ground of life. This is the peculiarly Western sense of sin, of radical and natural uncleanness in one's very vitals. The results of this are excessive and dangerous in two ways. On the one hand, it produces moral fanaticism, a fierce anxiety to be right, which, because it is an attempt to resolve an inner conflict of peculiar intensity, is often utterly blind to the injury that it does to other people. This is one of the many senses of the proverb that the road to hell is paved with good intentions, and it explains why wars fought in the defense of absolute moral principles are far more devastating and frightful than wars that spring from such ordinary human passions as greed.

On the other hand, inner conflicts in which one feels estranged from one's very nature can be so insupportable that the only escape seems to be by way of a violent reaction against the entire system of convention and theology that provokes them. When the mores are impressed upon us with too great a weight of authority, we are apt to turn against them with an acrimony that throws out the baby with the bathwater. And here we are no better off than before. It is really impossible to live in societies without moral conventions of some kind, for which reason these reactions never—save for the shortest periods—dispense with them altogether; the conventions are merely modified. In our culture, however, the baby that gets thrown out with the bathwater is God, the Absolute itself.

This has a very curious chain of results. God may disappear, but since the throne of the absolute is left vacant, its place is taken by the relative, by the conventions themselves, by society, or by the state. In fact, almost all revolutions swap a bad tyranny for a worse—Louis XVI for Robespierre, the czar for the Politburo. The same is true here. For when there is nothing absolute except the relative, when there is no higher

court of appeal, as it were, than social conventions and institutions themselves, the tyranny of convention is complete.
This accounts to a considerable extent for the absence and the
increasing disappearance of freedom in the two great secular
states of the modern world—Russia and the United States.

The Catholic Church always left the individual an "out"
from the fierce inner conflict between their own nature and
the divinely sanctioned order of society. Just and righteous
as God might be, God was always merciful. There was always
the possibility of release from guilt through confession and
absolution, and, in the last resort, the Church would always
admit that even in the case of those who died unregenerate
the extent of God's mercy and grace was unknown. Hell was
indeed a possibility, but never, in any individual case, a certainty. In this sense, the mercy of God, the unknown quantity,
one might say, the very unconventionality of God's justice,
has been the salvation of the Church—by reason of which it is
still something of a going concern. For this is the one respect
in which the Christian Church approximately resembles the
sort of institution for unlearning the conventions to which
I was referring. But even so, the individual could not lean
upon the divine mercy too heavily without entering into danger of the serious sin of presumption; and there are those for
whom the tension of uncertainty and doubt as to one's relation to God is more insupportable than knowing that you are
damned outright.

Thus the peculiarly and abnormally neurotic nature of our
Western societies is originally due, I think, to the fact that our

religious traditions provide no cure for one's upbringing, for the damage done in the necessary process of social discipline. To put it in another way, our religious traditions provide no adult initiation. For very many centuries the Christian initiation ceremony has been displaced. Baptism has been primarily a rite for children, conferred upon them at the beginning, instead of the end, of their period of constraint. Therefore it has altogether lost the character of an initiation into a mystery. I am inclined to believe that this could have happened only because there never really was a mystery to be initiated into, and there never was a mystery because God was never allowed to be really mysterious. That is to say, God was never allowed to be beyond the conventional boundaries of good and evil. God was inseparably allied with the good, with the conventional moral law.

This being so, there is obviously no place for a mystery. For it will by now be clear to you that in any real adult initiation, the mystery so closely guarded from the profane and undisciplined is precisely that the absolute is unconventional, that it is beyond good and evil, and that, by consequence, we *cannot* go against it or be separated from it. To put it in another way: the mystery is that the rules of society are not the laws of nature, and, furthermore, that the laws of nature—if we may call them that—are such that we could not go against them even if we wanted to. I will go further still: we cannot even *want* to go against them since we ourselves are the very process of those laws. There is no way to go against them as there is no way for the hand to strike itself. You may remember the words of Goethe's "Fragment Upon Nature": "We are encompassed by her, enfolded by her—impossible to escape from her and impossible to come nearer to her. The most unnatural also is nature. Who sees her not on all sides sees her truly nowhere. Even in resisting her laws one obeys them; and one works with her even in desiring to work against her."

You can easily see that this might be a very dangerous philosophy in the hands of an immature person. On the other hand, it is just as obviously a tremendous release for a person tied up in the clutches of a completely self-contradictory and insoluble inner conflict. A real understanding of this mystery is, furthermore, release from the whole insincerity and unnaturalness of self-consciousness. Of course, it is dangerous, but then everything is dangerous—food is dangerous, love is dangerous, life itself is dangerous!

But now comes a fascinating example of the inner identity of a revolution with what it revolts against. This particular mystery was not admitted by the moral absolutism of the Church. It is, if anything, even more inadmissible to the secular and absolutely relativistic philosophies that have replaced the Church. To the Church it was a dangerous and damnable heresy. But in the eyes of our modern absolute relativists it is completely meaningless—for they will tell you that words such as I have just quoted from Goethe cannot possibly correspond with any actual experience. They will insist that to see nature on all sides is to see her nowhere at all, since if nature means everything she means nothing. Experience, they will say, is necessarily a matter of contrasts and relations, so that what cannot be contrasted with something different from itself can never be an experience, just as light cannot be recognized apart from the contrast of darkness.

All this is very true if what we are talking about is language as distinct from experience, symbols and signs as distinct from reality. For the logical relations between words and ideas are such that certain expressions—such as "all events are natural"—do not convey any *verbal* information or meaning. But it does not follow that there is no experience to which these words correspond and that they express as well as words can. It is a very misleading confusion of words with reality to assume that what cannot be thought cannot be experienced, or, to put it the other way round, whatever can be experienced can be expressed in thought.

I have just discovered a passage in Aldous Huxley's *Texts and Pretexts* that puts this so perfectly that I want to read it to you:

> Our immediate impressions of actuality, on the rare occasions when we contrive to see with the eyes of children or convalescents, of artists or lovers, seem to have a quality of supernaturalness. What we ordinarily call "nature" and find duller than a witling's jest is in fact the system of generalizations and utilitarian symbols which we construct from our sensations. Sometimes, however, we are made directly and immediately aware of our sensations; it is an apocalypse; they seem supernatural. But it is through sensations that we come into

contact with the external world, the world of Nature with a capital N. Hence a seeming paradox: external Nature is supernatural; and the supernatural, because mental, universe in which we do our daily living is all too natural—natural to the point of dullness.

What he calls the "system of generalizations and utilitarian symbols that we construct from our sensations" is precisely the conventional system of institutions into which our upbringing fits us like the bed of Procrustes. Where we are too short, we are stretched; were we are too long, we are chopped off. But when this fitting process has gone on long enough, we need to be freed from it—and if this does not happen, we continue to confuse the world of symbols and conventions with the world of reality, of Nature. Herein lies the identity of the two opposed wisdoms of the West—of the Church and of the secularists, of the theologians and the positivists. Both have confused the conventional with the real—the one by identifying God with goodness, and the other by identifying the order of nature with the order of words, and this is one and the same mistake.

Now I am sure that a society can escape the more wildly insane consequences of this confusion if there is within it even a small minority of people who have been cured of, or liberated from, the necessary evil of their social conditioning. There is doubtless such a minority in our own world, but it has no status. Society does not recognize it—which is another way of saying that society does not recognize any limits, any sphere of life beyond its jurisdiction. This is why Thoreau complained that solitude is not really allowed, that men will pursue you to the ends of the earth to compel you to belong to their desperate company of oddfellows.

In more traditional societies than our own, the official philosophy or religion almost invariably had two aspects—the profane and the sacred, the outward and the inward. Outwardly, it collaborated in imposing the social and moral disciplines necessary for communal life. But inwardly, for the responsible initiates, it was concerned with the realm beyond good and evil, self and others, humanity and nature—the realm where relative and conventional rules and distinctions no longer apply. This is the realm of freedom from the bed of Procrustes, and of which the Buddhist poem speaks when it says:

> In the spring scenery nothing is better, nothing
>   is worse;
> The leaves grow naturally, some long, some short.

The lack of some such counter-discipline, some such cure for our being conformed and integrated with the group, is, from a long-range view, the single most conspicuous defect of modern societies. But I do not see how we are going to get it while our official religions are so afraid of it. Their principal fear is, of course, that it seems to undermine the guarantees and sanctions for moral conduct. But has it never occurred to them that the only really significant and authentic moral acts come out of freedom—and that seemingly moral acts that arise from constraint or fear or shame are strictly counterfeit? Nor do I see how we are going to get it when so many of the official schools of psychiatry are working for normalcy or adjustment, which, as Lewis Hill once pointed out, is simply another word for obedience. No, I am afraid it is the measure of our profound inner insecurity that we are so damnably tidy, that we cannot tolerate the presence of saints or lunatics, that we cannot really live with people who disagree with us about anything serious, that we conceal and avoid emotions, and make ourselves more and more into the semblance of Kipling's monkeys, the Bandalog, crying, "We all say so, so it must be true!"

5. The Art of Nonsense

I was talking to you last week about the necessity for being cured of our education, or upbringing. To be more exact—I should say being cured of the inevitable inner conflicts, the warpings, which our education involves. I was also talking about the fact that many cultures have recognized this necessity and have provided regular means whereby a certain number of people may be freed from the bondage of their social conditioning. This is not at all the same thing as destroying their entire education, as making them quite literally forget everything they have learned. This point is very important. Freedom from conditioning means to be able to use what you have learned without being bound by it. Let us put it in this way: the ordinary person is forced to learn the conventions of society, and thus learns to identify themself with them. They move within them like a train on its rails. But a liberated person is more like an automobile; they can, if they want, stay on a certain track—but they can also move away from it.

In various ancient or traditional societies, such as the Indian and the Chinese, institutions such as Buddhism or Vedanta or Taoism or Zen were the regular means for liberating people from the ill effects of their conditioning. I pointed out that Christianity has not, to any important extent, played the same role in the West—and for the reason that the Christian God or Absolute has been identified with the forms of social convention, with mores, and there has been a general fear of recognizing that God is beyond them. I pointed out, too, that this has weighted our conventions with an altogether excessive amount of authority, resulting in violent revolutionary reactions, which throw out the baby with the bathwater, or in paralyzing states of inner conflict.

This time, I want to discuss with you the actual process whereby a liberation from convention is achieved, a process that is entirely different from those merely reactionary revolutions that exchange one kind of tyranny for another, usually worse. But to understand this process, I think we must first understand that the most important part of our conventional upbringing is the training of the way in which we speak and think. For almost all conventions are conventions of communication—and this is why the word "code" applies equally to a system of laws or customs as to a system of signs, whether words or gestures, whereby we represent various events to other people or to ourselves.

In the total course of our education, from toddler to college graduate, we have been learning code. We have been learning the conventional signs for events and for the relationships between events. All of this has been a very difficult and often painful acquisition. Consequently we are apt to be extraordinarily touchy about it. We hate to have it called into question because it has cost us so much and represents so much effort. Hence all the excesses of cultural imperialism, of the conflicts arising from the insistence that our way of life—that is, our code—is the best way of life.

I was saying that the most important part of the code is the way in which we speak and think, that is to say, language, whether spoken out loud or uttered silently in the mind. The vast importance of language is perhaps best seen in the fact that people are most acutely frustrated when life does not make sense, when the order of events does not correspond with the order of thought. Few of us will have much objection to dying when we are eighty. But there is a great deal of objection to dying when we are eight. The first is natural, but the second is an accident, since it does not fit in with our preconceived idea, or thought, of order. How often, then, do we hear it said that it simply doesn't make sense that the life of so promising a child should have been cut short? It hardly needs to be said that events of this kind disturb us more profoundly than anything else.

In the same way, you can listen with relative comfort to a talk on the radio that makes sense according to the code of language. But supposing I were to address you in some such way as this:

"The withering spoon was fleet, and out of the matchless quantity of laminated bees, a cumbersome bench of spotted nails was derived with angular turrets. Suddenly a crowd of winged peppers was arraigned before a naturally dovetailed potato, and equal sections of fried popularity were sequestered on either roof, so that a marvelous rocket of scattering pigeons was amputated on the best behavior of a titillated squirrel."

Well, you might listen for a while for the sheer sense of novelty and incongruity. But if it went on much longer, you might begin to feel outraged and insulted and start calling up the station to get that lunatic off the air. Why? Because I am not making sense, I am not using the code of speech in a way that seems to correspond with any sort of reality in the natural universe. Yet I would be sorry if you were to dismiss this kind of utterance out of hand, because there is really quite an art to composing it, and the rationale of this art is intimately bound up with the process of liberation from conditioning. To understand this art, we must first recognize that there are a number of quite different kinds of nonsense—ranging all the way from mere balderdash to pure non-sense, which, if you analyze the word, has almost the same meaning as "supernatural"—what is beyond the senses, or better, beyond understanding.

This is rather an odd kind of inquiry, but may I give you examples of some quite different kinds of nonsense. There is first of all "lalling," the utterance of a series of meaningless and playful sounds. This is the very easiest kind of nonsense to talk:

Thrumular, thrumular, thrilp
Cum lipsible, lipsible lilp;
Dim thricken me thrummy
Lumgumptulous bummy;
Stormgurgle umbuMDITar bilp.

Then, rather close to it, is the nonsense of a series of words linked by the association of alliteration as distinct from the association of rationality. "Tell me a tale of tesselated, tintinabulating, tittle-tattling tonsilectomy." At a slightly higher level comes the nonsense in which words are linked, not by rationality, but by common association—common in the sense of general usage, or in the sense of frequent usage by the individual. "Fowls love feathers to develop photographically, and camaraderie is black with a blue wave, with hair all flying on a winged harp." Note the obvious associations of develop—photographically—camaraderie—black and blue—blue waves—wavy hair—hair flying—etc. These associations are harder to discover in a kind of nonsense where they are, consciously or unconsciously, arrested and concealed. Thus the association "black and blue" may become "black and blooming" and, to continue, "blooming with fluorescent illusions of

unredeemable privacy." Flowering became fluorescent, illumi-
nation became illusion, unreality became unredeemable, and
so forth.

Now all these kinds of nonsense are terribly easy to speak
or write. The really difficult kind of nonsense is to create,
without deliberation or hesitation, a series of words falling
out of the mind without *any* associations between them—
words following one another haphazardly as if they had been
drawn from a hat. I suppose there are people who will say that
this is impossible, and they can invariably prove their point
because you can find associations between any two words
whatsoever if you look hard enough. Wasn't it the Duchess in
Alice in Wonderland who said, "Meaning, dear? Anything has a
meaning if you only look for it!" So let me give you an example
of this highest and very difficult kind of nonsense. It is, of
course, a Zen story. Someone asked Joshu, "I read in the scrip-
tures that all things return to the One, but where does this
One return to?" The master replied instantly, "When I was in
the province of Tsing, I had a robe made that weighed nine
pounds." What connection, what relation is there between the
answer and the question? None at all.

This may sound easy, but it isn't. Our thinking is so dom-
inated by habit that it is actually quite difficult to give a completely dissociated and yet spontaneous answer to a question.
All this may sound like an invitation to the wildest insanity, yet
there is method in this madness, and it will, I think, become
clear if we consider the following quotation from another Zen
master, the celebrated Sixth Patriarch Huineng: "As thought

follows thought, do not think of past events. If the succession of our past, present, and future thoughts is incessantly linked by mutual connection, this is called being tied up in knots. But if, in the course of events, you do not dwell upon each succeeding thought, there will certainly be no knots."

Huineng describes the lack of inner freedom as the habitual and compulsive linking of our thoughts together, by association—rational or otherwise—into a chain. He is suggesting that we learn to break up the chain, to let thoughts follow one another haphazardly. Of course, if you are afraid for your own sanity, if you feel that rational thinking is a very precarious possession, this may not be a very sensible thing to try. But, once again, let me stress the point that this haphazard thinking is not intended to displace connected thinking; it is intended to counterbalance it, to make connected thinking an instrument that we use freely instead of a compulsive habit—to make us think connectedly and disconnectedly with equal facility.

To a very considerable extent, life itself helps us in this task insofar as the ordinary course of events is itself haphazard. In this case, all that is necessary to learn haphazard thinking is to follow the course of events. But the difficulty here is that we try not to see how haphazard this course actually is. Compulsively, we do our damnedest to make sense out of it. We do it by projection, reading connections into things by taking the advice of the Duchess: Anything has a meaning if only you look hard enough. We do it also by selection—that is, by paying attention only to those fragmentary aspects of events that can be made to fit together in a connected way. Indeed, what we call events are precisely such fragmentary aspects, for they are selected bits of experience. For an event is defined by excluding everything else that was happening at the same time. Or to put it in another way, any event is only a small part of itself! In reality, there are no fixed boundaries between the wave now breaking on Seal Rock and the rest of the Pacific Ocean. We can even say that the ocean is breaking on Seal Rock. It is perhaps less easy to see the same continuity between a person walking along a street and the street itself—as well as everything else going on in the street, not to mention the city where the street is located. The person walking is a selection from the rest of the experience, grasped as the focal point of attention.

Needless to say, this selection of connectable points is highly practical. It is like crossing a river filled with rocks— picking out just those rocks that can be used as stepping-stones. But as the connection between those particular rocks is the legs of the person crossing the river, so the connection between selected events is in the mind that picks them out— and in doing so finds a way across the river of life. In reality, in the state of nature, all those rocks are equally connected or disconnected—whichever way you want to look at it.

But there is a point at which picking out these stepping-stones ceases to be practical. This is when we come to believe that the connection between them lies in the stones and not in the mind, for as this belief becomes more and more firmly entrenched, we lose our ability to see that there may also be many other, and perhaps better, ways of crossing the river. So, too, our conventions, our codes of social communications are confused with laws of nature, and we become unable to change or improve them, and so lose our freedom.

Yet beyond this obviously practical disadvantage there is something still more momentous, and though less obvious, much more practical. The inner conflicts that arise from trying to fit the haphazard course of events into the patterns of "making sense" required by the code bring about an intense state of strain—all the more intense when we believe that these code-patterns are objective and real, like laws of nature. It is quite obvious that excessive emotional strains have a destructive effect. Less obvious is the fact that they conceal, or wipe out, a peculiar sensation of harmony—or one might say, naturalness—that would otherwise be our normal way of feeling. It is probably hard for most of us to imagine how we could feel natural or harmonious in the midst of a completely haphazard universe—a universe where making sense out of things is a kind of game like seeing pictures in an inkblot. But our difficulty lies in the fact that we have been taught to identify ourselves, our own lives and feelings, exclusively with order, with the code, so creating a fundamental conflict with spontaneous chance. This conflict would not arise if the identification of ourselves with order were less exclusive, less compulsive—though by no means something to be set aside altogether.

Hence the necessity of jolting our thinking out of the ruts in which it ordinarily runs, not to throw it into a new set of ruts but to give it the freedom to roam rutless, as well as in ruts. And what is needed, in the first place, is a clear intellectual understanding of the problem, a good theoretical grasp of the difference between conventions of thought and actual reality, between the order of words and the haphazardry of nature, between the abstract world of so-called facts and events and the concrete world of immediate experience.

Beyond this, our minds must learn to wander—not from association to association as in daydreaming, but rather in a high state of alertness, like a swordfighter defending themself from attack from all sides at once. This is a feat that we cannot perform if our alertness is strained to the point of paralyzing action. On the other hand, if our thrusts and parries come out in a regular order, lacking the element of surprise, our opponents will soon overwhelm us. But for the slight alliterative association at the beginning of the list, I would say that the best possible advice for us is that of the Walrus, for

> "The time has come," the Walrus said,
> "To talk of many things:
> Of shoes and ships and sealing-wax,
> Of cabbages and kings,
> And why the sea is boiling-hot,
> And whether pigs have wings."

Biting an Iron Bull

I suppose most of you have heard of Zen, but before going on to explain various details about it, I wish to make one thing absolutely clear. I am not a Zen Buddhist, I am not advocating Zen Buddhism, and I am not trying to convert anyone to it. I have nothing to sell. I am an entertainer. When you go to a concert and you listen to someone play Mozart, he has nothing to sell except the sound of the music. He does not want to convert you to anything. He does not want you to join an organization in favor of Mozart's music as opposed to Beethoven's. I approach you in the same spirit as a musician with her piano, or violinist with his violin: I just want you to enjoy a point of view that I enjoy.

Now, then, that has been said, and I hope it has put your minds at rest. Let me give you, first of all, some simple historical information. Zen is a form of Buddhism. It originated in China in about 500, and in about 1200 it was transmitted to Japan, where it exists today. It is a way of life that has had an immense influence on the arts, culture, poetry, and architecture of the Far East. Lately, it has become of enormous interest to many people in other parts of the world. Normally when one speaks about Buddhism, and Zen is a form of Buddhism, it is supposed that one is talking about a religion. People are apt to classify themselves as Buddhists much in the same way as they might say, "I am a Catholic, or a Methodist, or a Baptist, or an Episcopalian, or a Jew." This is rather misleading, however, because Buddhism is not a religion in that sense. If we want to find a equivalent to Buddhism in Western society today, the nearest thing is probably psychotherapy. We go to a psychiatrist or psychoanalyst to work out a serious personal problem. When we feel that our whole life is somehow disoriented and wrong, we do not go to a preacher, because a preacher only moralizes and says, "My man, you should have more faith in God." We go instead to a doctor, because in our day a person with the tag of science has more prestige than a person who has the tag of religion. When a psychiatrist goes to work on you, their objective is to change your state of consciousness. If your state of consciousness, your state of mind, is one of constant depression, the psychiatrist or psychotherapist's objective is to change your state of consciousness to happiness.

In a somewhat similar way, the objective of Buddhism in all its forms is to bring about a fundamental change in the human being's everyday state of consciousness. It is to bring about a change in one's sense of personal identity, your sensation of who and what you are. Buddhism is a method of changing consciousness discovered by a man called Gautama, who lived in India shortly after 600 B.C.E. and was given the title "Buddha"—"The Awakened One," "The Man Who Woke Up"— suggesting that ordinary people are asleep.

The problem to which the Buddha primarily addressed himself is suffering. Prior to exploring that, however, we have to be clear about certain basics, and these basics have to do not so much with concepts and ideas as they do with a state of mind. You could also call it a state of feeling, a state of sensation, or a state of consciousness; whatever we call it, we need to understand it before we can really proceed very far. It is an extraordinarily difficult state of mind to talk about, even though in its nature it is extremely simple.

The nature of this crucial state of mind is similar to our state of mind as an infant, when we had not been told anything and did not know anything other than what we felt, and we had no names even for that. As we grow older, of course, we learn to differentiate one thing from another and one event from another, but above all, ourselves from everything else. This is well and good, provided we do not lose the foundations.

The multiple things of this world are differentiated, but they have a shared basis, just as mountains are differentiated but they are all based on the earth. There is no word for that basis, not really, because words are only for distinctions, and so they cannot really even be a symbol, not even an idea, of the non-distinction. We cannot think it, but we can feel it, though we do not feel it like an object. You feel you are alive, you feel you are conscious, but you do not know what consciousness is because consciousness is present in every conceivable kind of experience. It is like the space in which we live, which is every-where. It is like a fish in water; the fish does not know it is in the water, because it never leaves it.

As we grow up and become fascinated, spellbound, and enchanted by all the things that adults wave at us, we forget the background and we come to think that all the distinctions that we have been learning are supremely important. We become hypnotized much in the same way as a chicken does when its beak is put to a chalk line. The chicken gets hung up, gets stuck on the line. When we are told to pay attention to "what matters," we get stuck on it, and this is what is called attachment in Buddhism.

Attachment does not mean enjoying food, sleep, or beauty. Those are responses of our organism, and they are as natural as feeling hot near a fire or cold near ice. Likewise, our responses of fear or sorrow are not attachment. Attachment is quite pre-cisely translated by the slang term "hang-up." It is a kind of "stickiness," or what is called "blocking" in psychology. We get hung up on all the various things we are told as we grow up by our parents, our aunts and uncles, our teachers, and above all by our peer group. The first things everybody wants to con-vince us of is the difference, the separation between ourselves and the rest of the world; and the distinction between those actions that are voluntary and those that are involuntary—what we do, on the one hand, and what happens to us, on the other. This is, of course, immensely confusing to a small child, because it is told to *do* all sorts of things that are really sup-posed to *happen,* like going to sleep, loving people, and not blushing. What occurs is this: the child is told in some way that we, your parents, elders, and betters, command you to do that which will please us only if you do it spontaneously. No wonder everybody is completely confused.

We go through life with that burden inside us, and we therefore develop this curious thing that is called an "ego." Now, an ego is not the same thing as a particular living organism. The organism is something real, though it is not a separate thing but a feature of the universe. On the other hand, what we call our ego is something abstract. It has the same order and kind of reality as an hour or an inch or a pound or a line of longitude. It exists for purposes of discussion, for convenience. The possession of an ego is a social convention; the fallacy that all of us succumb to is treating it as if it were a physical organism, as if the ego were real in that sense, when in fact it is no more than our image of ourselves. When we say to somebody, "You must improve your image," this image is not ourselves any more than the idea of a tree is a tree, any more that you can get wet in the word "water." Our image of ourselves is extremely inaccurate and incomplete. My image of me is not at all your image of me; in addition, my image of me is extremely incomplete. It does not include any information to speak of about the functioning of my nervous system, my circulation, my metabolism, my subtle relationships with the entire surrounding human and nonhuman universe. The image I have of myself is a caricature arrived at mainly through my interaction with other people who tell me who I am in various ways, either directly or indirectly. I play with their picture of me and they play something back to me, and we establish a shared conception of me. This started very early in life when I was told I must be me, and you were told you must be you, and that each of us must have a consistent image. We are encouraged to seek our identities in our images, and this is an awful red herring.

A lot of the current quests for identity among younger people are a search for an acceptable image. What role can I play? Who am I, in the sense of what am I going to do in life? While that search has a certain importance, it is extraordinarily misleading if it is not backed up by a deeper understanding of the natures of image and identity. On the one hand, we possess an intellectual, emotional, and imaginative image of ourselves; yet on the other hand, we feel that we are only images, and that there is something inside us more real than the images, a sort of sensitive core inside the skin and that corresponds to the word "I."

Let us take a look at this. The thing that we feel is "myself" is certainly not the whole body, because a lot of the body can be seen as an object. In other words, you stand, stretch yourself out, lie on the floor, turn your head, and look at yourself. You can see your feet, your legs, and your chest, but finally it all vanishes except for a vaguely seen nose in front. You assume you have a head, because everybody else does, and you have seen it in a mirror. But you can never see it directly, just as you cannot see your back. We tend to locate our egos in the unseen part of our bodies, the inaccessible part from which everything seems to come.

We believe we feel the presence of our ego, our "I-ness," but what is it we really feel? Let us compare the ego to the eyes. If I see clearly, and my eyes are in functioning order, they most certainly are not conscious of themselves or their working. There are no spots in front of them, no defects, and no awareness of "eye-ness." The parts of the eye—the lens, retina, and optic nerve—produce the hallucinations we know as vision without intruding their presence upon the process. By the same token, if my ego, my consciousness, is working, I ought not be aware of it; yet I am, as some sort of a nuisance, the thing that sits in the middle of everything. What is it, then, that we feel as our ego? Well, I think I have discovered that it is a chronic and habitual sense of muscular strain, which we were taught to do in the process of performing normally spontaneous things to order. When you are taking off in a jet plane, and the plane has gone rather further down the runway than you think it should have without getting up in the air, you may start pulling at your seat belt to get off the ground. Of course, this is perfectly useless. A similar thing happens when someone tells us to look carefully, to listen or pay attention. We start straining the muscles around our eyes, ears, jaws, and hands. We try to use our muscles to make our nerves work, which is of course futile and in fact hinders the functioning of the nerves. When we try to control our emotions, we hold our breath, pull our stomachs in, or tighten our muscles to "pull ourselves together." Of course tightening one's muscles is useless as a means of controlling one's emotions.

This chronic tension, which in Sanskrit is called *sankoca,* meaning "contraction," is the root of what we call the "feeling of the ego." The feeling of tightness is the physical referent for our psychological image. This ego is the marriage of an illusion to a futility. The idea of labeling a being with a name is naturally useful for social communication, provided we know what we are doing and take naming for what it is. We become so hung up on this concept, however, that it confuses us, and we do not imagine that it might be possible for us to feel otherwise. When we hear about a person who has transcended the ego, we ask, "How did you do that?" But the proper question is, "What do you mean by *you*?" The ego cannot be transcended, because it does not properly exist. You cannot do anything about a nonexistent thing, anymore than you can cut a cheese with a line of longitude.

Perhaps that sounds very discouraging, but let us suppose we are babies again, and we do not know anything. Don't be frightened, we'll get our knowledge back later; for now, let us pretend we are only awareness. Let us suppose that we have no information about ourselves at all and no words for the self, and that even my talking to you right now is just a nonverbal noise. Do not try to do anything about this. Do not make any effort, because by force of habit certain tensions remain inside you and certain words and ideas drift all the time through your mind, just as the wind blows or clouds move across the sky. Do not bother with them at all. Do not try to get rid of them: just be aware of what is going on in your head as if it were clouds in the sky or the crackling of the fire. This is not really difficult, and there is no trick to it: all you have to do, really, is look and listen without naming, and if you are naming, never mind, just listen to the naming.

You cannot force anything. You cannot willfully stop thinking, and trying to stop naming is only telling yourself that the separate "you" doesn't exist—it is not a mark of defeat or a sign of your lack of practice in meditation. It runs on all by itself, and simply means that the individual, separate "you" is a figment of your imagination.

You are aware at this point of a happening. Remember that you do not know anything about the difference between you and it. You have not been told that you have no words for the difference between inside and outside, between here and there. Nobody has taught you that what you see out in front of you is either near or far from your eyes. A baby puts out a finger to touch the moon and does not know its distance. It knows that it is here, and calls it "this." You will feel it, the "going on," which includes absolutely everything you apprehend. That is what the Chinese call Tao and Buddhists call suchness; it is a happening. It does not happen to *you,* because where is that "you"? What you call "you" is an aspect of the happening, which has no separate parts. At first this happening process may seem a little scary, because it had never occurred to us that a process could be self-controlling.

This spontaneous process going on we call "life," and it is controlling itself, aware of itself through you. You are an aperture through which the universe looks at itself, and because of the universe looking at itself through you, there is always an aspect of itself that it cannot see. It is just like a snake pursuing its tail, because the snake cannot see its head as the observer can. We always find, as we investigate the universe, ever more minute things; and as we make bigger and bigger telescopes, the universe expands. Why? Because it is running away from itself, in both directions. Now, it will not do that unless you chase it, so the universe is chasing its own tail. This is the Tao, a game of hide-and-seek. When you ask the question, "Who is doing the chasing?" you are still working under the assumption that every verb has to have a subject, and that when there is an action there has to be a doer. This is merely a grammatical convention, leading to what Whitehead called the "fallacy of misplaced concreteness," like the famous "it" as in "it is raining." So when one declares that there cannot be knowing without a knower, one is saying no more than there cannot be a verb without a subject; that, however, is a grammatical rule, not a law of nature.

Anything you can think of as a thing, as a noun, can be described by a verb, and there are languages that do so. When you look for doers as distinct from deeds, you cannot find them, just as when you look for stuff underlying the patterns of nature, you cannot find any stuff. Instead, you just find more and more patterns, because there never was any stuff; in fact it was a ghost all along. What we call "stuff" is simply pattern seen out of focus. When it is fuzzy, we call it stuff. We have these words—energy, matter, being, reality, even Tao— but we can never find them. They always elude us entirely, although we do have the very strong intuition that all this that we see, our universe, is connected or related.

The word "universe" really means "one turn"—and a short turn at that, for though you can make one turn to look at yourself, you cannot make two turns and see what is looking. As they say in Zen, you cannot take hold of it, but you cannot get rid of it, and in not being able to get it you get it. In fact, all these trials that gurus put their students through have as their ultimate object convincing the student—and convincing very thoroughly—that one cannot do anything. Even the gurus, however, can only convince you in a theoretical way.

Incidentally, I am not a guru, and I do not give individual spiritual direction to people. Instead, I give away the guru's tricks. That may not be nice, but, on the other hand, those tricks are only necessary in the sense that it is necessary for you to go to a psychiatrist if you think you must. You may not be satisfied unless you go to Japan and study Zen Buddhism with a *roshi,* but it is not necessary unless it is the only thing that will satisfy you. If you feel that need, you feel it. On the other hand if you do not, no one should think less of you. The point is, what do *you* want to do? What is in you to do? You can struggle and struggle, and indeed will do so as long as you have the feeling inside you that you are missing something. All sorts of people will do their utmost to persuade you that you are missing something, because they are missing something, and they think that they are getting it in a certain way. To assure themselves they have made the right choice, they would like you to do what they do.

Now, a clever guru beguiles their students by letting them have the feeling of success and accomplishment in certain areas. Therefore, a guru gives people exercises that are either difficult but can be accomplished or that are impossible. You will always be hung up on the impossible ones, but with the possible ones you will get the feeling of making progress, so that you will double your efforts to solve the impossible exercises. The guru arranges many levels through which you can advance to this stage of consciousness or that state of consciousness, much like the different belts you can earn in judo. This gives people the sense of competing with themselves, or even with others, all because of the feeling inside that they are missing something.

Of course, if you are learning any sort of skill and you have not perfected the skill, there is indeed something you are missing. But this is not true in Zen, because, as the Buddhists say, we are buddhas from the very beginning. All of that searching is like looking for your own head, which you cannot see and therefore might imagine you have lost. The point is simply that we do not see that which looks, and therefore we think we have lost it. We are in search of the self, the *atman*, but that is the one thing we cannot find because we have it, we are it.

Although you will think at first that this is a kind of determinism, there are two reasons why it is not. First, there is nobody being determined. People think of determinism as the direction caused by the past. If you use your senses, however, you will see that such strict causation is a hallucination. The present does not come from the past. If you listen, and only listen, where do the sounds come from? According to your ears, you hear them coming out of silence. The sounds come, and then they fade, and off they go like echoes in the labyrinth of your brain, which we call memories. The sounds do not come from the past; they come out of now and trail off. When we see our hands move, we see the hands, and then as they move, we think that the movement is caused by the hands and that the hands were there before, and so they can move later. We do not see that our memory of the hands is an echo of their always being, trailing off, echoing like the wake of a ship. Just as the wake does not direct the ship, the past does not move the present unless you insist that it does. If you say, "Naturally I am always moved by the past," this is an alibi, and it completely fails to explain how you ever learned anything new. For this reason, psychologists do not really understand learning, because according to the theory of learning everything new is really only assimilated when translated into terms of what you already know. If that were true, learning would be a library that increases only by the addition of books about books already in it (and indeed a lot of libraries are like that).

When you become aware that this happening is not happening *to* you because you *are* the happening, and the only you there is, is what is going on, you begin to disregard the stupid distinctions you have been taught. You experience the odd feeling of a synthesis between doing and happening, in which doing is as much happening as happening, and happening is as much doing as doing. If you are not very careful at that point, you will proclaim yourself God Almighty in the Judeo-Christian sense. Freud alleged that babies feel they are omnipotent, and in a way they are. I am omnipotent in so far as I am the universe, but in the role of Alan Watts, I am not omnipotent—perhaps only cunning.

This sensation of the happening is what we want to explore. It is simply there: we cannot do anything, and we cannot *not* do anything. It is important not to distract yourself, however, because if you do, you will miss what follows from the feeling of what is going on when you are not doing anything and when you are not able even to not do anything. This, you see, is the sticky place. You cannot get in, and you cannot get out, and that is why in Zen it is called "the mosquito biting the iron bull" or "swallowing the ball of red-hot iron," which we cannot gulp down and cannot spit out. It is that difficult.

What are you to do, or not do? The dilemma that you thought was you is simply not there at all. Now, do not make it difficult. That is a form of evading it. Do not make it easy. That is a form of evading it. It is neither difficult nor easy, because if it were difficult, it would have to be difficult for someone. If it were easy, it would have to be easy for someone, and the someone we are talking about is just the one that is not there. If you think it is there, okay, you can have that thought—but it is a thought. In other words, your ego is a thought among thoughts. It is not the controlling thinker, or the feeler, or the sensor. It is this thing that is going along, and we get anxious because we feel nobody is in control. But nobody ever was.

Taoist Ways

In the initial stages of Zen training, the master will discourage thinking. Although you may come to them with a lot of ideas, your difficulty is not going to be solved by ideas. It is not going to solved by talk and intellectualization, and so they are not encouraged. Intellectualization creates a gap or lack of rapport between you and your life. You may think about things so much that you get into the state where you are eating the menu instead of the dinner, you are valuing the money more than the wealth, and you are confusing the map with the territory. What the master wants to do is get you into the landscape, to get you into relationship with what *is* as distinct from ideas about what is. This is a very important preliminary discipline, but later on you may realize that the process of thinking is also what is, that thoughts in their own domain are as real as rocks and words have their own reality as much as sky and water. Thoughts about things are in their own turn things, and so they lead you eventually to the point where you intellectualize and think in an immediate way.

The philosophy of Tao sees humanity as a part of nature rather than dominating it. There are several well-known Chinese paintings with the title *Poet Drinking by Moonlight*. When you look at one of them, at first you see a vast landscape. Only after searching very thoroughly, almost with a magnifying glass, do you finally find the poet tucked away in a corner of the painting drinking his wine. If, however, the subject *Poet Drinking by Moonlight* were painted by a Western painter, the poet would be the central figure, dominating the whole picture, the landscape a mere backdrop. Of course some Chinese painters specialize in family portraits and paint very formal paintings of ancestors on their thrones, but the Taoist- and Zen-inspired painters view humainty as an integral part of nature. Humanity is something in nature, just as everything else is, including mountains and streams, trees, flowers, and birds. We are not commissioned by some sort of supernatural being to farm or dominate nature. The Taoists see nature as a self-regulating, self-governing, and indeed, democratic organism, with a totality. It all goes together, and this totality is the Tao.

When we speak in Taoism of following the course of nature, or following the way, what we mean is doing things in accord with the grain. This does not mean we do not cut wood, but that when we cut wood we cut along the grain, where the wood is most easily cut. In interacting with other people, we try to interact along the lines that are the most genial. This is the great, fundamental principle called *wu wei*, or "not forcing." *Wu wei* is often translated as "not doing," "not acting," or "not interfering," but "not forcing" seems to me to hit the nail on the head. We never force a lock because we will bend the key or break the lock. Instead we jiggle it until it turns. *Wu wei* means always acting in accord with the pattern of things as they exist. When we follow the principle of *wu wei*, we do not impose any kind of extraneous force on a situation, because such force, by its very nature, is not in accord with the situation. For example, the people living in an urban slum are in a bad situation. They need better housing. But if we simply go in and knock the slum down and put in its place some architect's imaginative notion of a superefficient high-rise apartment building to "store" these people as if they were goods, we do not solve the problem; we create utter chaos. The slum, for all its shortcomings, has an ecology of its own. It consists of a very complex system of relationships, which make it a going concern, even though it may not be going very well, and anybody who wants to alter that situation must first become sensitive to all the conditions and relationships involved.

It is terribly important to be aware of the interdependence of every form of life upon every other form of life. This is how, for example, we cultivate the animals that we eat. We look after them, and feed them, and see that they breed in reasonable quantities. We do not do it very well, as a matter of fact, and troubles are arising about the supplies of fish in the ocean and all sorts of things resulting from our poor or shortsighted husbandry. But in the greater ecology it is clear that the apparent conflict among various species is not actually a competition. Instead it is a very strange system of interrelationship, a system of things feeding on each other and cultivating each other at the same time. This is the idea of the friendly enemy, the necessary adversary who is part of life. You have conflicts going on in your own body. All kinds of microorganisms are eating each other up, and if that were not happening, you would not be healthy. All the interrelationships of nature, whether they appear to be friendly relationships, as between bees and flowers, or conflicting relationships, as between birds and worms, are actually forms of cooperation. This is called "mutual arising." When you understand this as the basis of all existence and are able to act "without forcing," your life is spontaneous, a life that is so of itself, natural, not forced, and not unduly self-conscious.

Now another term that is important, although it has greater use in Neo-Confucian philosophy and Buddhism than in the writings of Lao-tzu, is *li*. This is a very useful concept in understanding the sort of natural order of mutual interdependence and mutual arising. *Li* originally meant the markings in jade, the grain in wood, or the fiber in muscle. It is defined nowadays in most dictionaries as "reason" or "principle," but this is not a very good translation. Joseph Needham once suggested that "organic pattern" was an ideal translation, and this is certainly preferable. The markings in jade are regarded as what make it beautiful. As you look down at the water here, you see patterns in the foam when a wave breaks. As you watch those patterns, you know they will never make an aesthetic mistake. They are not symmetrical and they are very difficult to describe. They are wiggly, as are the markings in jade, and the grain in wood, which we also regard as beautiful. All these things exhibit *li;* they all have distinct forms that we can distinguish quite clearly from what we call a mess. The foam patterns of waves, the mineral patterns of jade, and the vegetable patterns of wood are extraordinarily orderly, yet they do not have an obvious order, and nobody can ever pin this organic order down completely. We know that it is order and that it is something quite different from a random mess, but there is no way of defining that order completely.

In order to be able to paint that way, or live that way, or to deliver justice that way, you have to have that order in you, innately. You have to have an essential sense of *li,* but there is no way of prescribing it. This is very difficult for teachers, because in all of our modern schools and universities, we are attempting to teach creativity. The trouble is that if we found a method whereby we could teach creativity, and everybody could explain just how it was done, it would no longer be of interest. The mysterious—the dark black of lacquer, the impenetrable and profound depth out of which glorious things come—is always an essential element in the creative. There is a poem that says, "When the bird calls, the mountain becomes more mysterious." Imagine that you are in a mountain valley and everything is silent; suddenly, somewhere off in the distance, an unseen crow caws. You do not know where the crow is, but its cry emphasizes the silence and creates an element of mystery. There is a Chinese poem written by a man who went to find a sage who lived in a little hut in the mountains, with a boy there to serve him: "I asked the boy beneath the pines. He said, 'The master has gone alone, herb gathering somewhere on the mount, cloud-hidden, whereabouts unknown.'"

The best teachers of athletic and artistic skills are those who teach without forcing. I once studied the piano, though I am absolutely no good at it now because I do not practice. But I had an absolutely superb teacher for a while. He was a very great musicologist and his standards were the highest. When I first went to him, he said, "Let me see what you can do." So I played a Scarlatti sonata, and he said, "The trouble with you is that you are trying too hard. You are hitting the piano, and you should never hit a piano. Actually, all you have to do in order to play a piano is to drop your hands on it, and so you need to have relaxed arms." He made me practice for a while and felt my muscles to see if I were relaxed or not, and then he said, "Now just drop your hands on the piano. I don't care which notes you hit, but just drop your hands, let them fall. There is enough energy in the weight in your arm to play as loud as you will or as soft as you will—just let them drop."

He kept feeling my arms. "No, no, you are getting too tense, you must pretend you are Lao-tzu," he said, for he was a very educated man and he knew about these things. Then he said, "Now, after dropping your hands all you have to do is hit the right notes." He continued, "You know, the same thing is involved in making a very complex trill," and he demonstrated. He just dropped his hand on the piano and at the same time his fingers went "flluump," and produced a magnificent ornamentation. We went on and we practiced this for some time, and then he said, "Now let's get around to hitting the right notes."

Let us return to the problem of thinking about thinking. Sometimes people are removed from life because they dwell in the world of the intellect. They are living in a world of symbols. Intellectuals are in a way removed from life, tied up in their categories and catalogs, their musts and must nots. Yet this realm is also real, and thinking about thinking can be lived with as much directness, freshness, and spontaneity as life without thinking. In order to live in the realm of thinking about thinking with full spontaneity, we must no longer regard the symbol, the thought, the idea, or the word as a block to life or a means of escape from life. To be able to use the symbol, but not as means of escape, you have to know that you cannot escape in the first place. Not only can you not escape, but there is no one to escape: there is no one to be delivered from the prison of life.

The liberation of the mind from symbols is exactly the same process as breaking up the links between successive moments and the illusion of a continuing self that travels from moment to moment. Such a continuing self is as much an illusion as a wave of moving water, or the appearance of a solid circle created by moving a cigarette in the dark. The fallacy of the continuous self is pointed out by the saying, "No one perceives anything, and no one experiences anything— there is simply seeing and experiencing." In fact we introduce these redundancies through language, when we talk about seeing sights, hearing sounds, and feeling feelings. There are sights, there are sounds, there are feelings. We do not feel a feeling; the feeling itself already contains the feeling of it. This is very simple. Sight does not depend on the existence of the seen and the seer, bound together by some mysterious process. The seer and the seen, the knower and the known, are what we call "terms." Terms mean ends, and these are in mathematical language called limits. Now, when we pick up a stick, the stick has two ends, and they are the terms of the stick. The ends of the stick do not exist as separate points that encounter each other on the occasion of meeting at a stick. Actually, they are abstract points, and the ends in and of themselves and considered as themselves are purely geometrical Euclidian imaginations; the stick is the reality.

In the same way, in the phenomenon called experience the reality is not an encounter of the knower and the known. The reality is the experience that can be termed as having two aspects, two ends, the knower and the known, though this is only a figure of speech. In a neurological sense, everything you see is yourself. What you are aware of is a state of your nervous system, and there is no other knowledge whatsoever. That does not mean that your nervous system is the only existing reality, and that there is nothing beyond your nervous system, but it does mean that all knowledge is knowledge of you, and that therefore, in some mysterious way, you are not different from the external world you know. If you see, then, that what you experience and what you are are the same thing, then take it a step further and realize also that you are in the external world you are looking at. Just as I am in your external world, you are in my external world, but I am in the same world you are. My inside is not separable from the outside world. It is something that the so-called outside world is doing, just as it is doing the tree, the ocean, and everything else in the outside world. Now, isn't that great! We have now completely eliminated the person in the trap, the one who either dominates the world or suffers under it. It has vanished, it never was there, and when that happens, you can play any life game you want. You can link the past, the present, and the future together and play roles, but you know that you have seen through the great social lie that one accumulates or owns experiences, whether memories, sights, sounds, or other people. We are always building up our self as the haver of all this, but if you think that, you have been had!

Swimming Headless

T *e*, the second word in the title of Lao-tzu's *Tao Te Ching*, presents us with some serious problems in translation. It is ordinarily translated "virtue," but virtue as we understand it today isn't at all appropriate. *Te* means virtue in the sense that we speak of the healing virtues of a plant. In the section of the Lao-tzu where the term is introduced the text reads, literally, "Superior virtue, not virtue, thus it has virtue. Theory of virtue cannot let go of virtue, thus it is not virtue." A smoother translations is, "Superior virtue is not conscious of itself as virtue, therefore it is virtue. The idea of virtue it is so hooked on being virtuous, that it is not virtue." *Te* means the excellence of things in the sense that a tree excels at being a tree. There is no way to imitate a tree; the only way is to be one. In the same way, when a human being shows extraordinary skill at something, it seems that it comes naturally to them. No artifice is apparent, and if there is some discipline involved, it is concealed. Such artless excellence seems like magic, and in *te* there is a connection between virtue and magic.

Everything is fundamentally in harmony with the Tao. It is said the Tao is that from which nothing can depart, and that from which things can depart is not the Tao. Fundamentally, then, we cannot escape it. It is as if we are all floating in a tremendous river, which carries us along. Some people may swim against the river, yet they are still being carried along. Others have learned the art of swimming with the river. They are carried along too, but they are aware of it. They know they are being carried along, whereas the people who are swimming against the river *think* they are going in the opposite direction, though they're not, really. We have to flow with the river; there is no other way. We can swim against it and pretend not to be flowing with it, but we still are. What's more, the person who gives up that pretense, who realizes one is inevitably carried by the river and swims with it, suddenly acquires behind everything they do the force of the river.

The person swimming against the river does not by their action express the power of the river. On the other hand the person swimming with it rides the river's force and has behind them the whole river, the power of which they can subtly direct. They can change direction in the river, going to the left or the right as a ship uses a rudder to steer in the current; or if they are more skillful still, they can tack. When a sailboat tacks, it sails against the wind, yet it still uses the wind to blow it along. That is the most skilled art of all; that is perfection in Taoism.

I remember once looking into the air, and one of those glorious little thistledown things came floating along. I picked it up,

like that, and brought it down, and it looked as if it were strug-
gling to get away, as if it were an insect caught by one leg. I first
thought "Well it's not doing that, it's just the wind blowing."
But then I thought again. "Is it really only the wind blowing?"
Surely it is the structure of this thistledown, which in cooperation with the wind, enables it to move like an animal—but
using the wind's effort, not its own. It is a more intelligent
being than an insect, in a way, because an insect exerts effort.
A person who rows a boat employs effort, but a person who
puts up a sail employs magic: with the intelligence to use a sail,
they let nature work for them. *Te* is a kind of intelligence that
creates cooperation, so that the desired end is accomplished
without unnecessary effort. For example, instead of forcing
others to agree with you, you can give them the notion that
the idea you want them to have is their own. When you want
to teach a baby to swim, you can put the baby in the water and
then move backward in the water and create a vacuum. This
pulls the baby along, and it learns the feel of the water and,
eventually, how to swim on its own.

The *Tao Te Ching* is a book written for several purposes. We
may take it as a guide to mystical understanding of the universe, or we may take it as a dissertation on the principles of
nature, almost a naturalistic handbook of natural law. We may
also take it as a political treatise, a book of wisdom for gover-
nors, and on this subject the basic principle that it advocates
is the virtue of governing by not ruling. Suppose the president
of the United States were as unknown to you by name as the
local sanitary inspector, the person who looks after the drains

and the sewage disposal. The inspector may not be a glamor-
ous figure, but for that very reason they probably do their job
more efficiently than the president. The president wastes an
enormous amount of time interviewing various groups, con-
ferring honors, and so forth, and with all of the ceremonial
functions, the poor person's life must be an utter torment.
They are so well known that they have little time to give to the
government of the country. Just think of their mail, and all
the people who have to be employed sifting it out and assess-
ing it. If they were someone quite anonymous, so that we did
not have to think about them, they would be a very good ruler
in just the same way, for example, as are the systems that gov-
ern your own body's functions. You do not have to attend to
your body unless you are sick. The government of your body
happens automatically, going on day after day after day. The
better it is, the less you have to think about it. On the deepest level, a person can get in the way of their own existence
by becoming too aware of themself. Such a person lacks the
quality of *te*.

The Taoists propose to help people get back to Tao and the
state of *te*, so that they will not get in their own way. The key,
they say, is the idea of being empty. Emptiness, being vacant,
is the secret of all things. The highest kind of knowledge is not
"know how" but "no how"—to be able to achieve things with
"no how," that is, without any method. This is done through
something called "fasting the heart." The Chinese word I
translate as "heart" does not mean heart in the physiological
sense. Pronounced *hsin*, it is in fact a part of the character *te*,

and its meaning is closer to "heart-mind" or "psychic center." *Hsin* is also frequently translated as "mind," and in all the Zen texts where the term "no mind" is used, the actual word is *wu hsin* (Japanese, *mushin*). The most desirable kind of heart, then, is absence of heart. In English, "heartless" has very bad connotations, as does "mindless." A heartless person is an inconsiderate and unfeeling person, and a mindless person is an idiot, but in Chinese Buddhism and Taoism, a person who has *mushin,* no mind or no heart, is a person of a very high order. Their psychic center does not get in its own way, and it operates as if it were not there.

Lao-tzu said that "the highest form of man uses his *hsin* like a mirror—it grasps nothing, it refuses nothing, it receives but does not keep." And the poem says, "When the geese fly over the water and they are reflected in the water, the geese do not intend to cast their reflection and the water has no mind to retain their image." The art of living is to operate in the world as if you were absent. As a matter of fact, this is built into us physiologically. Let me ask you simply: What is the color of your head from the standpoint of your eyes? You feel that your head is black, or that it has not any color at all. Outside you see your field of vision as an oval because your two eyes act as two centers of an ellipse. But what is beyond the field of vision? What color is it where you can't see? It is not black, and this is an important point; there is no color at all beyond your field of vision. This little mental exercise gives us an idea of what is meant by the character *hsuan*. Although its dictionary definition is "dark, deep, obscure," it actually refers to this kind of no color that is the color of your head—as far as your eyes are concerned. Perhaps we could say that the invisibility of one's head, in a certain sense the lack of a head, is the secret of being alive. To be headless (to have no head in just the sense I am talking about) is our way of talking about the Chinese expression *wu hsin,* or "no mind."

As a matter of fact, if you want to see the inside of your head all you have to do is keep your eyes open, because all that you are experiencing in the external, visual field is a state of your brain. All the colors and shapes you see are the way in which the brain nerves translate the electrical impulses in the external world outside the envelope of the skin. They translate all of what is going on outside into impulses that are to us shape and color. However, shape and color are states of the nerves, so that what you see when your eyes are open is how it feels inside your head. You do not see your brain as an internal undulating structure, you see your brain as everything outside. In this way the emptiness of one's head is the condition of seeing and the transparency of the eye lens is the condition of seeing colors. The thirteenth-century mystic Meister Eckhart said, "because my eye has no color it is able to discern color"; this is a restatement of the fundamental Taoist idea of being absent as a condition of being present, being not there so as to be there. Lao-tzu says, "When your belt is comfortable you don't feel it, when your shoes are comfortable it is as if you were not wearing any." The more aware you are of these things, the less well they are made or the less well they fit.

We may raise a very simple objection to this, which is that if I do not know I am there I seem to be missing everything. We want to know that we know. If we are happy and we do not know we are happy, we might just as well not be happy. To know that you are happy, is really the overflowing of the cup of life. The downside of this principle is to be miserable and know that you are miserable. Some people are miserable without knowing it, but you know my limerick:

There was a young man who said, though
It seems that I know that I know
What I would like to see
Is the I that knows me
When I know that I know that I know

Of course this is the great human predicament, the development of self-consciousness, the development of the possibility of reflecting upon one's own knowledge, which is simultaneously a blessing and a curse. Taoism does not escape this problem and it does not avoid this problem. It deals with it, but it does not deal with it obviously; it floats lightly over it.

Lao-tzu said, "It is easy enough to stand still; the difficulty is to walk without touching the ground." He is referring to the fact that in the state of being in accord with the Tao there is a certain feeling of weightlessness parallel to the weightlessness that people feel when they float in space or when they go deep down into the ocean. This is of course connected with the sensation that you are not carrying your body around, which

I compare to the experience of an expert driver when they really are "with it" in a car. When the hill lifts them up and drops them off the other side, there is a sense of weightlessness, and they and the road are all one process. This state is connected to the inner meaning of Lieh-tzu riding in the wind. When D.T. Suzuki was asked what is it like to have *satori,* he said, "It is just like everyday, ordinary experience except about two inches off the ground." Then of course there is the song, "Walking on air, never a care, something is making me sing, tra-la-la-la, tra-la-la-la, like a little bird in spring."

What is this weightlessness? It means that you are not moving around in constant opposition to yourself. Most people move in constant opposition to themselves because they are afraid that if they do not oppose themselves all the time they will lose control and something awful will happen. When the human being developed the power to be aware of themself, to know that they know—in other words when the cortex was formed over the original brain—they fell from grace. That was the fall of humanity, because when we felt the sensation of being in charge, of being in control of ourselves, we became anxious. Am I aware enough of myself? Have I taken enough factors into consideration? Have I done all that should be done? When we asked these questions of ourselves for the first time, we started to tremble, and this was the fall of humanity. This is also what Lao-tzu means when he says, "When the great Tao was lost there came duty to man and right conduct." In other words, nobody talks about how you ought to behave unless things have gone radically wrong.

There would not be any conception of faithful ministers of the state unless there were a lot of lousy politicians around. No one would talk about filial piety unless there were wayward sons and daughters. According to the Taoists, moral preaching is the source of confusion. There is a marvelous story about a conversation between Confucius and Lao-tzu in which Lao-tzu asked Confucius to explain to him about charity and duty to one's neighbor. In reply Confucius gave him a little sermon on giving up self-interest and working for others, to which Lao-tzu replied, "What stuff sir! Regard the universe. The stars come out invariably every night, the sun rises and sets, the birds flock and migrate without exception, all flowers and trees grow upwards without exception. With your 'charity' and 'duty to one's neighbor,' you are just introducing confusion into the realm. Your attempt to eliminate self is a manifestation of selfishness. You are like a person beating a drum in search of a fugitive." All talk about selfishness and all talk about becoming virtuous or enlightened or integrated or non-neurotic or self-actualized attests to the fact that it has not happened, and such talk will in fact get in the way of its happening.

The Taoist sage Lieh-tzu, who lived somewhat later than Lao-tzu, was known for his ability to ride on the wind. Before acquiring this skill, Lieh-tzu found a very great master and went to study with him. The master lived in a small hut, and Lieh-tzu sat outside the hut but the master paid absolutely no attention to him. Of course this is the way with Taoist masters. Why would they want students, since they have nothing to teach? After a year of sitting outside, Lieh-tzu went away because he was fed up with waiting so long. Then he became regretful about leaving and thought he really should make an attempt, so he went back to the master. When the master saw him approach, he asked, "Why this ceaseless coming and going?" So Lieh-tzu sat there and tried to control his mind so that he would not think of the difference between gain and loss, so that he could live in such a way that nothing is either an advantage or a disadvantage.

There is a marvelous story about this perspective. Once upon a time there was a Chinese farmer whose horse ran away, and all the neighbors came around to commiserate that evening. "So sorry to hear your horse has run away. This is most unfortunate." The farmer said, "Maybe." The next day the horse came back bringing seven wild horses with it, and everybody came back in the evening and said, "Oh, isn't that lucky. What a great turn of events. You now have eight horses!" And he said, "Maybe." The next day his son tried to break one of these horses and ride it but he was thrown, and broke his leg, and they all said, "Oh dear, that's too bad," and he said, "Maybe." The following day the conscription officers came around to conscript people into the army and they rejected his son because he had a broken leg. Again all the people came around and said, "Isn't that great!" And he said, "Maybe." The farmer steadfastly refrained from thinking of things in terms of gain or loss, advantage or disadvantage, because one never knows. Receiving a letter from a law office tomorrow saying that some distant relative of yours has left you a million dollars might make you feel very happy, but the windfall may well lead to unbelievable disaster—including a visit from the Internal Revenue Service, just to mention one possibility. In fact we never really know whether an event is fortune or misfortune, we only know our ever-changing reactions to ever-changing events. The Taoist is wise enough to understand eventually that there is not any fixed good or bad; this point of view is called non-choosing.

To return to Lieh-tzu. He attempted to keep his mind in a state of non-choosing, but it is very difficult to overcome one's habits of feeling and thinking. After he had practiced this for a year, the master looked at him and recognized he was there. After another year's practice, the master invited him to come and sit inside his hut. Then something changed, and Lieh-tzu did not try to control his mind anymore. He described what he did: "I let my ears hear whatever they wanted to hear, I let my eyes see whatever they wanted to see, I let my feet move anywhere they wanted to go, I let my mind think of whatever it wanted to think, and it was a very strange sensation because all my bodily existence seemed to melt, and become transparent, and to have no weight. I didn't know whether I was walking on the wind or the wind was walking on me."

We insist, however, that there are events; we observe events, we remember events, and they make an impression on us. Yet in the psychology of Taoism there is no difference between the observer and what is observed. We are only the observation of life from a certain point of view. We create an opposition between the thinker and the thought, the experiencer and the experience, and the knower and the known because we think about knowledge in terms of certain metaphors—the metaphor of the stylus on the writing sheet, the reflection on the mirror. All those sorts of images are part of our idea of knowledge, but the Taoist theory of knowledge is quite different. There is no knower facing the known, and if there is any knower at all, it contains the known. Your mind, if you have one, is not in your head; instead, your head is in your mind, because your mind, understood from the standpoint of vision, is space. The Chinese use the word *kung,* which means sky, space, or emptiness. *Sê* means both shape and color. The famous lines of the *Heart Sutra* declare that "Space/emptiness *is precisely* shape/color and shape/color *is precisely* space/emptiness." What we call space contains the myriads of shapes and colors and bodies and weights and so on. It does not reflect them as a mirror; but it is the absence that guarantees their presence and it is their presence that guarantees absence. There is a mutual arising between voidness and form, between existence and nonexistence, being and non-being, and these are never felt as alternatives or elements that are in some kind of contest. When we say, then, that there is not any thinker behind thoughts, nor any experiencer that has experiences, this is a way of saying that experiencing or knowing is not an encounter between strangers.

Western thought concentrates very much on knowledge as an encounter and talks about facing facts, facing reality, as if somehow or other the knower and the known came from two completely different worlds and met each other. The phenomenon of knowledge is almost the precise opposite of that. Instead of being a collision between two wandering bodies in space, knowledge is much more like the expansion of a flower from its stem, where stem and flower are knower and the known, the terms of something that lies between them. We tend in all our metaphors and common speech to think of life as a process that has polarized itself, coming out from a center and expressing itself in terms of opposites. Of course this is the basis of the whole yang/yin principle illustrated as two interlocked fishes. It is a fascinating emblem because it is a helix, and it is the formation of a spiral nebula, and it is the position of sexual intercourse. I am trying to get to the middle of you, you are trying to get to the middle of me, neither one of us exist without the other. The yang is the light and yin is the dark. Yang originally meant the sunny south side of a mountain, and yin the dark north side. Yang is the north bank of a river that gets the sun, yin is the south bank that is in the shade.

Now, there are no mountains with only one side. The mountain, if it is a mountain at all, goes up and down, like a wave. There are no waves with a crest but no trough or a trough with no crest, because you cannot have half a wave. Yang and yin are quite different from each other, but just because they are different they are identical, and this is the important idea of the "identical difference." The saying in both Taoism and Buddhism is that "difference is identity, identity is difference." The Chinese word for "is" is not quite the same as our word. It somewhat resembles "that," so we

might render the statement "difference that identity, identity that difference." This does not mean quite A *is* B, but that
A *is in relation to* B or A *goes with* B, or A *necessarily involves*
B. Difference necessarily involves identity, identity necessarily involves difference, so there is no yang without yin, and
there is no yin without yang. When I was first studying these
things, I was terribly bothered by how on earth I was going to
see this multi-differentiated world as a unity. What was going
to happen, what was it going to be like to see that all things
are one? The sages keep saying all things are one, but they
all look so different to me. All these people act in different
ways, and they have all their houses and their cars and all
their this and that. The whole world looked full of the most
bony, prickly differences. I thought, "Well, what is supposed
to happen? Is this supposed to be as if your eyesight blurred
and all these things floated together? What is this experience
of nirvana or of liberation supposed to be? Why do the Hindu
sages write about it just as if it were a kind of dissolution
of everything?" It took me a long time, and suddenly one
day I realized that the difference I saw between things was
the same thing as their unity, because differences, borders,
lines, surfaces, boundaries do not really divide things from
each other at all, they join them together, and all boundaries
are held in common. It is like a territory that has all been
divided up into property, and this is your property, and this is
my property. But if I live next to you, your fence is my fence,
and we hold the boundary in common. We may make up silly
arrangements as to who is responsible for the maintenance

of this fence, but nevertheless we hold our boundaries in common, and we would not know where my plot of land was unless we knew the definition of your plot of land, and the plot of land that is adjoining. I saw then that my sense of me being me was exactly the same thing as my sensation of being one with the whole cosmos. I did not need to have some other sort of different, odd kind of experience to feel in total connection with everything. Once you get the clue, you see that the sense of unity is inseparable from the sense of difference. You would not know your self, or what you meant by self, unless at the same time you had the feeling of other.

Now the secret is that the other eventually turns out to be you. The element of surprise in life is when suddenly you find the thing most alien turns out to be yourself. Go out at night and look at the stars and realize that they are millions and billions of miles away, vast conflagrations out in space. You can lie back and look at that and say, "Well, surely I hardly matter. I am just a tiny little speck aboard this weird spotted bit of dust called Earth, and all that was going on out there billions of years before I was born and will still be going on billions of years after I die." Nothing seems stranger to you than that, or more different from you, yet there comes a point, if you watch long enough, when you will say "Why that's me!" It is the other that is the condition of your being your self, as the back is the condition of being the front, and when you know that, you know you never die.

Zen Tales

All of us need to be liberated from our culture to a certain extent, largely because education is a kind of a necessary evil. When the process of education or acculturation has been completed, we need a cure for it. Education is like salting meat in order to preserve it; when we are actually ready to cook the meat and eat it, we need to soak some of the salt out. In the process of being brought up by parents and teachers, we are made tolerable to live with on the one hand, but on the other hand we are unavoidably damaged. As a result, in our culture, it is increasingly popular to undergo psychoanalysis after we complete our education, to work out all the damage and traumatic shocks we experienced in the process. In sophisticated circles psychoanalysis has become something one goes through not because one suffers from a specific mental sickness but because it is considered generally beneficial to mental health. Here we can see our fumbling attempt to find a cure for our own culture.

We need a cure because we lose our spontaneity in the course of being brought up. What is so delightful about children, as well as so objectionable, is that they are completely spontaneous. When we watch a child who is really just dancing for fun, we say, "That's delightful." The child eventually notices that this is a way of getting attention and becomes self-conscious about dancing. For our part, we send them to dancing school where they becomes stiff and wretched, and only after many, many years of practice does the child, now a young man or woman, recapture the spontaneity of childhood as a dancer. The child has gone the long way around to get back to the thing they once had, and of course it is terribly difficult to accomplish this at all.

The same is true of the "civilizing" process, of learning to live, as our culture teaches it. Each child is taught that he or she has to observe rules, and as we come to grips with that fact, something arises that bugs us human beings beyond belief: self-consciousness. Self-consciousness is, in one sense, our distinction as human beings, and it also contributes to our great ability to appreciate things. We not only have the ability to experience happiness, but we can know we are experiencing happiness. We not only think, but we can think about thinking and analyze the very capacity of reason. To think about thinking, to know about knowing, to be aware of what one does and hears, is the birth of rational control of behavior, which, we might say, is the glory of civilization. The glory of humanity is, however, its bane at the same time. How do we know when to stop thinking about thinking, for instance? You think about a problem, and you have to make a decision, but how long should you think about it? How much evidence should you collect before you act? You never know. What most of us do is to think about a decision until further thought is a nuisance. Then, when it is too late to think about it anymore, we act.

We never are sure that we decided the right thing, and one of the troubles about thinking about decisions is that there are ever so many unpredictable variables. You may work out the most perfect business contract, satisfied that you have covered every contingency you could anticipate—but you did not bargain for slipping on a banana skin on the way to your partner's office! Such a thing could not be predicted by any amount of analysis, and the more we try to elaborate perfectly foolproof methods of arranging our lives, the more we find ourselves encumbered with impossible details. This is also the fallacy of too much regulation by law. When we try to make the law provide for everything, suddenly we cannot move without filling out dozens of forms, or without consulting all sorts of bureaucrats and hiring a staff of lawyers and accountants. We take all kinds of measures to be sure we do not make the wrong move, but after a while the game ceases to be worth the candle, and life becomes so safe that it is not worth living at all.

This is one of the problems of becoming self-conscious, and all education is an instruction in self-consciousness. What do you learn in education? You learn words—symbols about reality—and with those words you become able to talk about living, to think about living, and to have knowledge about living. Knowledge is not academically respectable knowledge unless it is knowledge in terms of words or in terms of numbers, that is to say, in terms of a symbolic language about life. Once we know that we know, and we know we are alive and we know we are going to die because we can anticipate our futures, we feel that we have lost our innocence and something has gone wrong.

The whole problem of self-consciousness is that it puts us in a perennial dither and doubt, which we call anxiety. In response, we develop a nostalgia for an age of innocence, a time before self-consciousness. Wouldn't it be nice not to have to make any decisions, to act entirely on whim? If one got into trouble, that would be all right, because at least one would not have been anticipating it and worrying about it. When a moth mistakes a candle for its sexual object, the moth makes a mistake, and that is that. It does not worry on the way to the candle whether it is going to get burned, and of course moths are sufficiently prolific so that one moth more or less lost in a candle does not matter; hundreds of moths lost in candles do not matter: Moths just go on. We might imagine a human civilization where people make mistakes, and when they do, they go off with a glorious bang instead of a continual whimper, and that is that. They would not worry and they would live magnificently.

But we cannot possibly go back to such a state of innocence. One cannot give up self-consciousness on purpose, one cannot give up worrying, and one cannot give up thinking about oneself. So we remain terrified to live spontaneously, because we might do something wrong. The core of Zen training, however, is to live spontaneously, and this is why it is so fascinating to many Western people, and especially Western intellectuals, who are overburdened with self-consciousness. What fascinated people most about Zen when they first heard of it through Dr. Suzuki's writings were the Zen stories he introduced to them.

Years and years ago, I lent a book of Zen stories to a friend of mine. He was in the hospital, and when he gave it back to me, he said, "I didn't understand a word of it, but it cheered me up enormously." Tang dynasty China, from about 600 to 900, marks the golden age of Zen, and the Zen literature from that period is especially fascinating. It consists mostly of anecdotes about the encounters of Zen masters with their students. In Japanese, these are called *mondo*, which means "question and answer," and from the *mondo* that have come down to us, it appears that the way of studying Zen in those days was rather unlike it is now. Today Zen is an established religion and is studied in various settled communities, but in those days Zen was a wandering practice. When you became a Zen monk, you did a great deal of traveling; instead of sitting on your fanny most of the day, you trudged. You were walking along across prairies, up mountain paths, through rugged country, and you were visiting master after master after master to find one who would answer your question.

We must imagine a seeker, not a phony seeker, but a true seeker. They have within them a burning desire to find out what it is all about, who they are, what life is, what reality is. What is the way out of this mess? Instead of remaining a mixed-up human being, they want to become something as simple as a tiger, or a cat, or a bird, or a buddha. Such seeker-monks used to wander and wander in search of someone who would answer their questions.

One of the oldest Zen stories is of a man who came to where Bodhidharma was meditating. Bodhidharma refused to see anybody, and the man who came to see him was refused like all the others. Finally, the seeker cut off his left arm and presented it to the master to prove his seriousness. Bodhidharma said, "All right, what do you want?" The man said, "I have no peace of mind. Please pacify my mind." The Chinese word is *hsin,* which is often translated as "mind," but is not actually the same. *Hsin* is a more inclusive word meaning the heart-mind, the center of psychic activity. When you say "I have no peace of mind," it doesn't mean you just have a headache; you have a heartache, too. Bodhidharma said to this man, whose name was Akar, "Bring out your mind before me and I will pacify it," and Akar said, "When I look for my mind, I cannot find it." Bodhidharma replied, "There, it's pacified now." And this answered Akar's question.

All Zen stories are like this. They are similar in nature to jokes. A joke is told to make you laugh. Laughter is not an intellectual thing, it is an emotional reaction, and the point of the joke is to stir that emotion. If the joke has to be explained to you, you may chuckle out of politeness, but you will not laugh spontaneously, you will not laugh from your belly.

Of course, the object of Zen is not to produce laughter, but to produce awakening, clarification, enlightenment, or what is called in Japanese *satori*. Like laughter, *satori* is something that happens suddenly. As a rule, one does not begin to laugh gradually, first softly and then louder and louder. You see a joke instantly. A joke is a matter of an "aha!" The Zen stories are also intended to produce an "aha!" reaction in you, a "But, I see, now it's clear." They do not in fact contain any information. They are not designed to tell you something, to impart information or knowledge. They are designed to get rid of something, to make a false problem with which you are wrestling disappear. In the story of Akar and Bodhidharma, understanding equaled the disappearance of the problem; when Akar looked for the mind that was giving him so much trouble, he could not find it.

The stories are often quite astonishing, and I would like to tell a few. Some are quite well known, but I will try and choose ones that are less familiar.

One day a Zen master was walking in the forest with a group of his disciples. Suddenly he picked up a tree branch and said to one of the monks, "What is it?" The monk hesitated, so the master whacked him with the branch. Then he turned to another monk, and said, "What is it?" The second monk replied, "Give it to me so I can see." The master tossed him the branch, and the second monk caught it and hit the master with it. "You got out of that dilemma!" cried the master.

On another occasion, an officer of the army came to a Zen master and said, "Sir, I have heard a very strange riddle and I want to hear your answer to it. Once upon a time there was a man who kept a goose in a bottle, and it grew so large that he couldn't get it out. Now, he didn't want to break the bottle, and he didn't want to hurt the goose, so how did he get it out?" The master changed the subject, and said something like, "It's a nice day today. Isn't the waterfall making a lovely sound outside?" So they went on in pleasant conversation, and when the officer got up to leave and walked to the door, the master said, "Oh, officer," and he turned around and said, "Yes?" The master said, "There, it's out!"

The famous Zen master Suibi Mugaku was in a lecture hall, surrounded by monks studying, when one of them approached him and asked, "What is the secret teaching of Buddhism?" Mugaku replied, "Wait until there is no one around, and I'll tell you." Later in the day, the questioner accosted him and said, "There is nobody around now. What is the secret teaching of Buddhism?" Mugaku led the monk into the garden and pointed at the bamboo. The monk said, "I don't understand." Mugaku remarked, "What a tall one that is, what a short one that is," and the monk was awakened.

There was a monk named Gotai, and whenever people came to ask him a question about Buddhism he would hold up a finger. That was the only answer he would give. Now Gotai had an attendant, and one day somebody came to the temple to inquire about the teaching being given there. The master was apparently out, and the attendant held up a finger. But actually the master was there, observing this exchange from behind a screen. When the visitor left, he came out of hiding and asked his attendant, "What is the fundamental teaching of Buddhism?" The boy held up a finger. Instantly the master drew a knife and cut the finger off. The boy was very dismayed and rushed away yelling. The master shouted after him, "Hey! Come back!" The boy returned, and the master asked, "What is the fundamental principle of Buddhism?" The boy went to hold up the finger, but it was not there, and he was enlightened.

A monk left his old master to study with a new one, and when he approached the new master, the master asked, "Who did you study with before you came to me?" The monk replied, "Oh, I studied with so and so." "What did he teach you?" "When I asked about the fundamental meaning of Buddhism, he answered me, 'Ting-Ting (the Chinese god of fire) comes for fire.'" "Well," the master said, "that was an excellent answer, but I bet you didn't understand it." "Oh yes, I understood it, because Ping-Ting is the god of fire, and if Ping-Ting should ask for fire, that would be like me asking about Buddhism, because I am really a Buddha already." The master shook his head and said, "I knew it. You missed the point completely." "Well, how would you deal with it?" asked the monk. The master said, "You ask me." So the monk repeated the question, "What is the fundamental principle of Buddhism?" "Ping-Ting comes for fire," replied the master, and the monk got the point.

I could go on with these stories indefinitely, but you will notice within them a certain shared dynamic. As a rule, they require a solution to a dilemma, or they do something that creates what we would call a "state of blockage." This is achieved by setting up a situation in which the participant anticipates one response, but then the master suddenly changes the rules, requiring a reaction different from the "normal," automatic response. If somebody passes you in the street and says, "Good morning," you say, "Good morning." You are not being spontaneous; in fact you are being nearly automatic. However, when somebody comes up to you and says, "Are you saved?" or "Do you accept Jesus Christ as your personal savior?" the unexpectedness of the question stalls or "blocks" most people. It's as if someone suddenly asked you, "Why have you got such long toenails?" when you are wearing your shoes and nobody can see your toes.

Anything that disrupts the normal flow of interchange may put you off-balance, and the object of Zen is never to be off-balance. To be off-balance is the real meaning of what is called *bonno* in Japanese, which means "entanglements" or "attachments," and is often translated as "worldly attachments." In Buddhist philosophy, enjoying your dinner is not regarded as a worldly attachment. That is natural. It is not a worldly attachment to need to sleep. That is perfectly natural, too. To be afflicted by worldly attachment is to be *sticky,* that is, to be like a wheel that sticks on the axle and squeaks. We are sticky when we are self-conscious, when we are, as we would say, "all balled-up" or "all clutched-up." We have lost our original spontaneity, and we are not flowing with the stream of the Tao, the course of nature, or whatever you want to call it.

The questions of the Zen *mondo* put you in a dilemma, and the point is to see if you can get out of the dilemma without a moment's hesitation. Without a moment's hesitation does not necessarily mean quickly, because being in a hurry to give an answer is itself a form of attachment. In this connection, you should all read in [D. T.] Suzuki's book *Zen and Japanese Culture* a letter written by the Japanese monk Takuan. He wrote a letter on the art of swordsmanship in which he explained the necessity of spontaneity. In swordsmanship, you have no time to stop to think how you are going to respond to an attack; at that moment, it is already too late and you are dead. You must respond as spontaneously as sound arises when you clap your hands, without a moment's hesitation; or as instantaneously as the spark flies when one strikes steel on flint. Takuan cautions that *trying* to be quick, however, will be a block to achieving quickness. The apprentice swordsman is first set to work as a sort of janitor for their master, working around the house and doing chores. The master takes every opportunity to surprise the apprentice, leaping out and hitting them with a bamboo sword when they least expect it. The apprentice is expected to defend themself immediately with whatever is available—a cushion, a broom, a saucepan, or anything they happen to be holding.

It soon becomes rather nerve-wracking going about one's daily work expecting to be jumped any minute, especially if one is always wondering where the next blow will come from. One soon discovers that the more one plans and anticipates the next attack, the more one will always be outwitted. The teacher is infinitely clever and will always come from an unexpected direction. Finally, one arrives at the point where one just gives up. One stops anticipating and relaxes; if one is hit, one is hit. Now at last the apprentice is ready to begin fencing. They have given up protecting themself, and therefore they have learned true defense; one cannot defend oneself by calculation, by linear thinking, by thinking one thought at a time when your enemy may attack from an infinite number of directions.

Another example of this kind of story is that of a woodcutter and a creature named the Satori. The woodcutter was working in a clearing in a forest, when he looked up and saw a strange animal peeking at him from behind a bush. Thinking to have the animal for dinner, he rushed at it with his ax, but before he could strike, the Satori laughed from the opposite side of the clearing. The creature had the power to read thoughts, and so he knew in advance from where the woodcutter intended to strike. After several attempts, the woodcutter began to grasp the Satori's powers, and naturally thought, "When I see him next, instead of going to where he is, I will go to the opposite side of the clearing." As soon as the woodcutter thought this, though, the Satori appeared at his side and mocked him: "So this is where you think I'm going to be next!" The Satori's taunting continued until the woodsman became absolutely furious and returned to chopping wood. The Satori laughed and said, "Ah, so you have given up." Just at that moment, as the woodcutter whacked the ax against the tree, its blade flew off and struck the Satori dead. And that is the way you have to attain Zen.

Likewise, the apprentice who studies swordsmanship is put into an impossible situation, in which they can do nothing right. After finding out that nothing will prevent them from being hit, they give up—and at last they can be spontaneous. Zen training is a discipline that is spontaneous within limits. In society, this is not possible, because people will be bugged if you say exactly what you feel and always act according to the truth. You will not be liked, and you may indeed do things that threaten your own safety and liberty. Zen training, however, is set up so that there is a walled-in situation in which one is allowed to be spontaneous within certain limits. The crucial moment of this training is what is called *sanzen,* a formal interview between student and master. In the climax of that interview, no holds are barred. It is a personal interchange where fundamental honesty is the crux of the exchange, and it is a very sticky situation, because the more you wonder how you are going to be fundamentally honest, the more you will get cold feet.

Supposing you were allowed an interview with God, and you were allowed to ask one question: What would you ask? If you think it over, you know it has got to be really important: it has to be the fundamental question. What is it that I really want to know? So you start thinking and thinking about that, but the more you think about it, the more you do not know what you would ask. You think, "That's a silly question, I know what she would say to that." You may think, "That is curious, an interesting question, and I don't suppose anyone knows the answer to it, but after all, it's only idle curiosity, so I don't think I'll ask that one." Then you might think of another question, and think about it for a while, and before long you realize that it is a question that does not mean anything, that it would be a waste of breath and a great opportunity, and so you continue this process of self-questioning and dismissal until you have considered all the questions you might ask. Visiting a great Zen master is very much the same. What are you going to ask them? You have just this one chance, so what do you want to know?

I remember a friend of mine who went to see a *roshi,* and when he got there, he said, "You know, I feel so silly, I haven't got any questions to ask you, I just feel like laughing." The *roshi* said, "Good, let's laugh," and he broke into a great roar. There are many facets of Zen that are so easily misunderstood just through reading about them. There is one school of people who tend to emphasize the spontaneity of Zen, and think, "This is great stuff. It means you may just do anything you like." It is true that certain of the great Zen masters have said that Zen is an art, and Rinzai made this point very strongly. He said that in Zen there is no place for discipline, or for Buddhism, or for making efforts of any kind. You just eat when you are hungry, sleep when you are tired, move your bowels when nature calls. Fools will laugh at me, he said, but the wise will understand. However, when somebody goes to Japan to study Zen, they write back home letters about hours and hours of sitting in one position, of being banged about with warning sticks and having to get up at the ghastly hour of four o'clock in the morning, wash in cold water, eat a very spare diet, and do everything according to a strict code. In Japanese Zen monasteries, austerity is the rule, and the visitor thinks, "What's going on?" "Is Zen this, or is it utter spontaneity?" The answer is that it is both.

Zen is a discipline, especially because in Japan today most Zen monks are not in the monastery because of any personal religious search, and have not been for hundreds of years. They have been there because it was a family tradition. In all traditional cultures in Asia, there is a tendency for the son to carry on his father's business. If you are a son of a priest, it is expected that you will be one as well, and so off to the monastery with you. It was the same in England in the eighteenth century, where one son went into the army, one son went into law, and one son went into the ministry. As a result a great many people without the slightest interest in religion ended up in theological school, and lacking real interest they had to be taught how to think. Saint Ignatius, for example, devised methods of meditation designed to teach people how to think even if they were not interested in thinking.

A great deal of monastery life, both in Europe and the Far East, is therefore designed to discipline people who have no genuine personal motivation for their religious training. One of the crucial points of Zen training is to develop within yourself what is called a "great doubt," and the *koan* is used to develop a great doubt. For example, the novice is asked to hear the sound of one hand clapping. Now in the case of the American student of Zen, he or she has probably come from far away and taken a good deal of trouble and expense to study Zen. Something personal, in fact, drove them to study Zen, and that something is the seed of the great doubt. To such a student, it seems terribly important to find the answer to the *koan*, and the more puzzled they are, the more a matter of life and death it seems. This student has roused a great doubt— they have an urgent spirit of inquiry—but cannot resolve it. The master keeps saying, "Come on, let's go! Be ready to give your life for this." And the student keeps at it.

But one who enters a Zen monastery because their family expects them to does not have that spirit of inquiry; they are just one of the children in the neighborhood brought up to enter the monastery. To them the teacher may say, "The trouble with you is that you don't have a great doubt." And of course this student does not have a great doubt—they are not even interested in what it may be! Eventually, however, they learn to cultivate a great doubt, but unfortunately great doubt cannot be made to order. In fact, it is difficult to do anything to order. This is the paradox of the discipline of Zen training.

There is a Zen poem that says, "You may want to ask where the flowers come from, / But even the god of spring does not know." Another poem says, "Planting flowers to which the butterflies come, / Bodhidharma says 'I do not know.'" All of what I would call "vital knowledge," or "living knowledge," is a mystery to itself. Life is a mystery to itself for the same reason. A Zen poem is "like a sword that cuts but does not cut itself, like an eye that sees, but does not see itself." The poem is saying that what truly exists, the most fundamental reality, knows itself and at the same time does not know itself. If it did know itself, it would cease existing, for, as in any game, if you know the outcome there is no point in playing it out.

When master chess players sit down and it becomes apparent, although there are still many pieces on the board, that one of them is going to mate in three moves, they quit. They are not bound to finish the game, because they know the outcome. If we knew the future perfectly and knew everything that we were going to do right up to the day of our death, we would say, "Why bother? Let's commit suicide and start another life." There is no point living through what is known completely. Of course, on the other hand, you cannot very well live through what is completely unknown either. There must be some light, but total light annihilates itself.

There can be no prescription and no infallible technique for teaching Zen, although indeed there are Zen schools. Sometimes the teacher who has many years of experience begins to get disillusioned. What is the point of all these schools? You cannot teach Zen; you can only pass it on from one person to another by osmosis.

In learning to play music, we must of course acquire techniques, but real mastery depends upon what we do with that technique. A person who is sufficiently motivated, who is fond of music, will study techniques because they're interested and they wish to master their instrument. Likewise, a person who is really interested in self-knowledge—and after all, Zen is only a way of acquiring self-knowledge—will master certain Zen techniques because they are interesting. Soon, however, the schools and systems begin to rely entirely upon techniques, because technique is the only thing you *can* teach. You cannot teach the thing itself!

When the student realizes that mastering techniques is not itself sufficient, that there is something that can't be taught and can't be learned but can only be experienced, they may panic. What if, after studying and mastering all these techniques, they don't get it? Different teachers have different things to say about this predicament. One may say, "Well now, look. Just forget about it. It does not matter if you don't get it. Not getting it is getting it." This paradox is used all the time. Not to have it, and to really accept that you do not have it—now that is getting it. In fact, that's the real point. "I am going to try as hard as I can *not* to try to get it." Here we are really playing a game. We think that in paradox we have found an infallible method, and we are convinced there must be an infallible method, for without a method, we are lost, we are up the creek.

But paradox is not the solution, either, and when we find out that there is no method, that there is no positive method and there is no negative method, what can we do? We cannot do something and we cannot do nothing. Nor can we just forget our dilemma, because by now we are preoccupied with it. This is what is called having "swallowed a ball of hot iron." You cannot gulp it down and you cannot spit it out. Zen is a trap to make you swallow a ball of hot iron.

We must be very careful how we proceed here, because we do not wish to end up in a padded cell blathering insanely. Yet this is the maddening quandary Zen confronts us with, which is why ever so many conflicting things can be said about Zen. On the one hand, it can be said rightly that Zen is a strict discipline, and on the other hand, it can be said rightly that it is not a discipline at all. Nor is it just a mixture of things, for Zen is not partly discipline and partly spontaneity. Whatever is said about part of it can be said of all of it, and therefore it seems to be paradoxical. There is no way of putting your finger on this thing, there is no way of nailing it down, and that's the whole point.

Zen makes you do what you were doing all the time, only it makes you do it consistently. Here is me and here is knowing about me. I want to try and control myself. I want to get a hold of that thing that is me, because when I get hold of it then I can control, and if I can control it everything will be all right. We are constantly doing this, and as a result, we have astounding illusions, including the illusion of separateness. We have that particular illusion because it is drilled into us through acculturation that each one of us is a separate ego and separate center of awareness. We see ourselves as a little living pulp of some kind that lives in a strange world that scares the heck out of us.

How did we ever come to imagine that we are somehow disconnected from what is out there, surrounded by a world in which we are strangers? It is quite obvious that this is not really so, although it is not obvious to most people. It is apparent that you, the real deep you, is this thing. That is reality, but you are having a profoundly interesting game pretending you are not it. You are going through all kinds of amazing mazes to play this game, hiding in terror from your own shadow, jumping at the sound of your own heart beating, and having goose pimples rise on your own back at the sound of your own footsteps. You are always exploring this world, and as you do, you find that it gets stranger and stranger. As you look out into the infinitudes of space where you thought everything was pretty rational, you see other galaxies that are millions of light-years away. You may think, "Well there are just a lot of galaxies out there." Suddenly, a quasar turns up, and nobody understands what a quasar is because the phenomenon defies all the things we thought we knew. So the universe grows stranger and stranger, and the more you probe it with your mind, the less you know. But when we recognize that all of this is nothing but our self, in myriad aspects, familiar and unfamiliar, we say, "Why, that's me!"

What a relief, and what fun to begin all over again.

Zen Bones

Once upon a time, there was a Zen student who quoted an old Buddhist poem to his teacher:

The voices of torrents are from one great tongue.
The lions of the hills are the pure body of Buddha.

"Isn't that right?" he asked. "It is," said the teacher, "but it's a pity to say so." It would be much better if this occasion were celebrated with no talk at all. If I addressed you in the manner of the ancient teachers of Zen, I should hit the microphone with my fan and leave. But I have the feeling that since you have contributed to the support of the Mountain Zen Center in expectation of learning something, a few words should be said, even though I warn you that by explaining these things to you I shall subject you to a very serious hoax. Now, if I allow you to leave here this evening under the impression that you understand something about Zen, you will have missed the point entirely. Zen is a way of life, a state of being, that is not possible to embrace in any concept whatsoever. Any concepts, any ideas, any words that I shall put across to you this evening will have as their object showing the limitations of words and of thinking. If one must try to say something about what Zen is, and I want to do this by way of introduction, I must emphasize that Zen in its essence is not a doctrine. There is nothing you are supposed to believe in, and it is not a philosophy in our sense; that is to say, it is not a set of ideas, an intellectual net in which one tries to catch the fish of reality. Actually, the fish of reality is more like water: it always slips through the net, and in water, when you get into it, there is nothing to hang on to. Of course all this universe is like water; it is fluid, it is transient, it is changing. When you are thrown into the water after being accustomed to living on the dry land and you are not used to the idea of swimming, you try to stand on the water. You try to catch hold of it, and as a result you drown. This refers particularly to the waters of modern philosophical confusion, where God is dead, metaphysical propositions are meaningless, and there is really nothing to hang onto because we are all just falling apart. The only way to survive under those circumstances is to learn how to swim; you relax, you let go, and you give yourself to the water. You have to know how to breathe in the right way, but then you find that the water holds you up, and indeed in a certain way, you become the water.

If one attempts (again, I say, misleadingly) to put Zen into any sort of concept, it simply comes down to this: that in this universe there is one great energy and we have no name for it. People have tried various names for it, such as God, Brahman, and Tao, but in the West the word God has so many funny associations attached to it that most of us are bored with it. When people say, "God the Father Almighty," most people feel funny inside, and so we like to hear new words. We like to hear about Tao, about Brahman, and about *tathata,* and other strange names from the Far East because they do not carry the same associations of mawkish sanctimony and funny meanings from the past. Actually some of the words that the Buddhists use for the basic energy of the world really do not mean anything at all. The word, *tathata,* which is Sanskrit for "suchness" or "vastness," really means something more like "da-da-da," based on the word *tat,* which in Sanskrit means "that." In Sanskrit existence is described as *"tat tvam asi,"* "That thou art," or in modern American, "You're it." But da-da is the first sound a baby makes when it comes into the world because the baby looks around and says, "da, da, da, da, da." "That, that, that, that, that!" Fathers flatter themselves and think their baby is saying "da-da" for "daddy," but according to Buddhist philosophy all this universe is one da-da-da, which means ten thousand functions, ten thousand things, or one suchness, and we are all one suchness.

Suchness comes and goes like everything else because this whole world is an on and off system. The Chinese say it is the yang and the yin and therefore it consists of now you see it, now you don't; here you are, here you aren't. It is the very nature of energy to be like waves, and of course waves have crests and troughs. However, we, being under a certain kind of sleepiness or illusion, imagine that the trough is going to overcome the wave or the crest; the yin, the dark principle is going to overcome the yang, or the light principle, and that off is finally going to triumph over on. We "bug ourselves" by indulging in that illusion. "Supposing that darkness did win out, wouldn't that be terrible?" We are constantly worrying and thinking that it may, because after all, is it not odd that anything exists? It is most peculiar, it requires effort, it requires energy, and it would be so much easier for there to have been nothing at all. Therefore we think that since being, since the *is* side of things is so much effort, we will give up after a while and sink back into death. But death is just the other face of energy. It is the rest, the absence of anything around that produces something around, just as you cannot have solid without space, or space without solid.

When you wake up to this, you realize that, as the French say, the more it changes, the more it is the same thing. You are really a playing of this one energy and there is nothing else but that. It is you, but for you to always be you would be an insufferable bore, and therefore it is arranged that you stop being you after awhile and then come back as someone else altogether. When you find that out, you become full of energy and delight, and as Blake said, "Energy is eternal delight." Suddenly, you see through the whole sham of things and you realize you are that and you cannot be anything else, so you are relieved of fundamental terror. Of course, this does not mean that you are always going to be a great hero, that you will not jump when you hear a bang, that you will not worry occasionally, or that you will not lose your temper. It means, though, that fundamentally, deep, deep down within you, you will be able to be human and not a stone buddha. In Zen, there is a distinction made between a living buddha and a stone buddha. If you approach a stone buddha and you hit it hard on the head, nothing happens except you break your fist or your stick. If you hit a living buddha, they will say "Ouch," and they will feel pain, because if they did not feel something, they would not be a human being.

Buddhas are human. They are not *devas,* they are not gods. They are enlightened men and women, but the point is that they are not afraid to be human. They are not afraid to let themselves participate in the pains, difficulties, and struggles that naturally go with human existence. The only difference is, and it is almost an undetectible difference, it takes one to know one. As the Zen poem says, "When two Zen masters meet each other on the street they need no introduction. When thieves meet they recognize one another instantly." So, a person who is a real cool Zen understander does not go around saying, "Oh, I understand Zen," "I have *satori*," or "I have this attainment or that attainment," because if one said that, they would not understand the first thing about it. Chuang-tzu said, "The perfect man employs his mind as a mirror; it grasps nothing, it refuses nothing, it receives but does not keep." Yet another poem says of wild geese flying over a lake, "The wild geese do not intend to cast their reflection and the water has no mind to retain their image." In other words, to put it in the contemporary idiom, this is to live without hang-ups. The word "hang-up" is almost an exact translation of the Sanskrit *klesha,* ordinarily translated as "worldly attachment."

All that sounds a little bit pious, and in Zen things that sound pious are said to stink of Zen. To have no hang-up, however, is to be able to drift like a cloud and flow like water, seeing that all life is a magnificent illusion, a playing of energy, and there is absolutely nothing fundamentally to be afraid of. You will be afraid on the surface, you will be afraid of putting your hand in the fire, and you will be afraid of getting sick, but you will not be afraid of fear. Fear will pass over your mind like a black cloud that flows through space without leaving any track. The stars also do not leave trails behind them. That fundamental clarity is called the "void" in Buddhism, which does not mean void in the ordinary sense of emptiness. It means the void that is the most real thing there is, though nobody can conceive it. The relation between the void and the world is like that you have between the speaker in a radio and all the various sounds that it produces. On the speaker you hear human voices, you hear every kind of musical instrument, honking of horns, the sound of traffic, the explosion of guns, and this tremendous variety of sounds is the vibrations of one diaphragm, but it never says so. The announcer does not come on first thing in the morning and say, "Ladies and gentlemen, all the sounds that you will hear subsequently during the day will be the vibrations of this diaphragm, so do not mistake them for reality." The radio never mentions its own construction, and in exactly the same way you are never able really to make your mind an object of your own examination, just as you cannot look directly into your own eyes and you cannot bite your own teeth. You are your mind, and if you try to find it and make it something to possess, it shows that you do not really know you are it. If you are it, you do not need to make anything of it because there is nothing to look for, but the test is, are you still looking? Do you know that?

This knowing is not a kind of knowledge that you possess, not something you have learned in school, not something a degree testifies to. In this knowledge there is nothing to be remembered and nothing to be formulated. You know it best when you say, "Well, I don't know it," because that means you are not holding on to it and trying to cling to it in the form of a concept. There is absolutely no necessity to do so, and should you try, you would be, in Zen language "putting legs on a snake" or a "beard on a eunuch," or as we would say, "gilding the lily." This sounds pretty easy, doesn't it? You mean to say all we have to do is just relax? We do not have to go around chasing anything anymore, we abandon religion, we abandon meditation, we abandon this, that, and the other, and just go on and live it up any way we like. This is what a father says to a child who keeps asking, "Why, why, why?" "Why did God make the universe?" "Who made God?" "Why are the trees green?" The father says finally, "Oh shut up and eat your bun." But it is not quite like that. All those people who try to realize Zen by doing nothing about it are still trying desperately to find it and are on the wrong track. There is another poem that says, "You cannot attain it by thinking, you cannot grasp it by not thinking," or you could say, "You cannot catch hold of the meaning of Zen by doing something about it, but equally you cannot see into its meaning by doing nothing about it." Both are in their different ways attempts to move from where you are now, here, to somewhere else. The point is that we come to an understanding of what I call "suchness" only through being completely here, and no means are necessary to be completely here, either active means on the one hand or passive means on the other, because in both ways you are trying to move away from the immediate now.

It is difficult to understand language like that, however, and to understand what it is about, there is really one absolutely necessary prerequisite, and that is to stop thinking. Now, I am not saying this in the spirit of being an anti-intellectual, because I think a lot, talk a lot, write a lot of books, and am a sort of half-baked scholar. Yet, you know that if you talk all the time, you will never hear what anybody else has to say, and therefore all you will have to talk about is your own conversation. The same is true for people who think all the time, and I use the word "think" to mean talking to yourself, subvocal conversation, the constant chitchat of symbols and images and talk and words inside your skull. Now, if you do that all the time, you will find that you have nothing to think about except thinking, and just as you have to stop talking to hear what others have to say, you have to stop thinking to find out what life is about. The moment you stop thinking, you come into immediate contact with what Alfred Korzybski called so delightfully, "the unspeakable world"—that is to say, the nonverbal world. Some people would call it the physical world, but these words "physical," "nonverbal," and "material" are all conceptual, and it is not a concept. It is not a noise either; it is simply this.

So, when you are awake to that world, you suddenly find that all the so-called differences between self and other, life and death, pleasure and pain, are all conceptual and they are not there. They do not exist at all in that world that is simply this. In other words, if I hit you hard enough, "Ouch" does not hurt. If you are in the state of what is called "no thought," there is a certain experience, but you do not call it "hurt." It is like when you were small, and children banged you about and you cried and they said, "Don't cry," because they wanted to make you hurt and not cry at the same time. That is the reason why there is in Zen the practice of *zazen* or sitting Zen. In Buddhism they speak of the four dignities of humanity, walking, standing, sitting, and lying; and incidentally, there are three other kinds of Zen besides *zazen*: standing Zen, walking Zen, and lying Zen. They say, "When you sit just sit, when you walk just walk, but whatever you do, do not wobble." In fact, of course, you can wobble if you really wobble well.

When the old master Hyakujo was asked what Zen is, he said, "When hungry, eat. When tired, sleep." His questioner countered, "Well, isn't that what everybody does? Aren't you just like ordinary people?" "Oh no," he said, "They don't do anything of the kind. When they are hungry they don't just eat, they think of all sorts of things. When they're tired they don't just sleep, but dream all sorts of dreams." I know the Jungians will not like that, but there comes a time when you just dream yourself out, and there are no more dreams, and you sleep deeply and breathe from your heels. That is what makes *zazen* or sitting Zen a very good thing in the Western world. We have been running around far too much. It is all right because we have been active and our action has achieved a lot of good things. Yet, as Aristotle pointed out long ago, and this is one of the good things about Aristotle, "The goal of action is contemplation." In other words, busy, busy, busy, but what is it all about? When people are busy, they think they are going somewhere and that they are going to get somewhere and attain something. There is quite a point to action if you know you are not going anywhere, and if you act like you dance, or like you sing, or play music, then you are really not going anywhere. You are just doing pure action, but if you act with the thought that as a result of action you are eventually going to arrive at some place where everything will be all right, then you are on the exercise wheel of a squirrel cage, hopelessly condemned to what the Buddhist call *samsara*, the round or rat race of birth and death, because you think you are going to get somewhere. You are already there, and it is only a person who has discovered that they are already there who is capable of action. That person does not act frantically with the thought that he or she is going to get somewhere, and can go into walking meditation at that point, where we walk not because we are in a great hurry to get to a destination, but because the walking itself is great and the walking itself is the meditation. When you watch Zen monks walk, it is very fascinating, because they have a different kind of walk from everybody else in Japan. Most people shuffle along, or if they wear Western clothes, they race and hurry like we do. Zen monks have a peculiar swing when they walk, and you have the feeling they walk rather the same way as a cat. There is something about it that is not hesitant, they are going along all right, but they are walking just to walk, and one cannot act creatively except on the basis of stillness, of having a mind that is from time to time capable of stopping thinking.

The practice of sitting may seem very difficult at first, because if you sit in the Buddhist way, it makes your legs ache and most Westerners start to fidget because they find it very boring to sit for a long time. However, the reason they find it boring is that they are still thinking, because if you were not thinking, you would not notice the passage of time. As a matter of fact, far from being boring, the world when looked at without chatter becomes amazingly interesting. The most ordinary sights and sounds and smells, the texture of shadows on the floor in front of you, all these things *are,* without being named and without saying, "That's a shadow, that's red, that's brown, that's somebody's foot." When you do not name things any longer, you start seeing them, because when a person says, "I see a leaf," immediately one thinks of a spearhead-shaped thing outlined in black and filled in with flat green. No leaf looks like that; no, leaves are not green. That is why Lao-tzu said, "The five colors make a man blind, the five tones make a man deaf."

If you can only see five colors, you are blind, and if you can only hear five tones in music, you are deaf. If you force sound into five tones and if you force color into five colors, you are blind and deaf. The world of color is infinite, as is the world of sound, and it is only through stopping fixing conceptions on the world of color and sound that you really begin to hear it and see it. The discipline, if I may be so bold to use that word, of *zazen* or meditation lies behind the extraordinary capacity of Zen people to develop such great arts as the gardens, the tea ceremonies, the calligraphy, and the grand painting of the Song Dynasty and of the Japanese *sumi-e* tradition. Especially in the tea ceremony, or *chanoyu,* which in Japanese means "hot water for tea," Zen masters found magic in the very simplest things of everyday life. In the words of the poet Ho Koji "Marvelous power and supernatural activity, drawing water, carrying wood."

Do you know how it is sometimes when you repeat a word until you make it meaningless? Take the word "yes." Yes. Yes. Yes. Yes. Yes. Yes. Yes. Yes. Yes. It becomes funny. That is why they use the word *mu* in Zen training, which means "no." If you say this word for a long time and the word ceases to mean anything, it becomes magical, and that is sound. The easiest way to stop thinking is first of all to think of something that does not have any meaning. Now, of course my point in talking about *mu* or "yes" or counting your breath or listening to a sound that has no meaning is that it stops your thinking because you become fascinated by the sound. Then, as your concentration continues, there comes a point when the sound is taken away and you are wide open. At that point there will be a kind of preliminary so-called *satori,* and you will think,

"Wow-wee, that's it!" You will be so happy that you will be walking on air. When Daisetsu Suzuki was asked "What is it like to have *satori*?" he said, "Well, it is like ordinary everyday experience except about two inches off the ground." There is another saying that the student who has attained *satori* goes to hell as straight as an arrow. Anybody who has a spiritual experience, whether one gets it through *zazen* or through anything that gives you that experience, if you hold on to it, and say, "Now I've got it," whist . . . it is gone, out of the window, because the minute you grab a living thing it is like catching a handful of water. The harder you clutch, the faster it squirts through your fingers, and there is nothing to get hold of because you do not need to get hold of anything; you had it from the beginning.

Of course, you can realize this experience through various methods of meditation. The trouble is the people who come out of that experience and brag about it. They say, "I've seen it." Equally intolerable are the people who study Zen and come out and brag to their friends about how long they sat and how much their legs hurt, and what an awful thing it was. The discipline of Zen is not meant to be something awful, and it is not done in a masochistic spirit with the puritanical outlook that suffering is good for you. When I went to school in England, the basic premise of education was that suffering builds character, and therefore all senior boys were at liberty to bang about the junior ones with a perfectly clear conscience because they were doing them a favor. It was considered to be good for them because it was building their character. As a result of this kind of attitude the word "discipline" has begun to stink, and it has been stinking for a long time. However we need an entirely new attitude toward this discipline, because without its quiet and non-striving, life becomes messy. When you finally let go, you have to be awfully careful not to melt and become completely liquid, because there is nothing to hold on to.

When you ask most people to lie flat on the floor and relax, you find that they are full of tensions, because they do not really believe that the floor will hold them up, and therefore they are holding themselves. They are uptight and they are afraid that if they do not do this, even though the floor is supporting them, they will suddenly turn into a puddle and trickle away in all directions. On the other hand there are people who, when you tell them to relax, go limp like a rag. Now, the human organism is a subtle combination of hardness and softness, of flesh and bones. The side of Zen that has to do with neither doing or not doing, but knowing that you are it anyway and you do not have to seek it, that is Zen flesh; but the side in which you can come back into the world with an attitude of not-seeking and knowing you are it and not fall apart, that requires bones. Acquiring Zen bones is one of the most difficult things.

A certain generation we all know about caught onto Zen and started an anything-goes painting, an anything-goes sculpture, and an anything-goes way of life. I think we are recovering from that today. Our painters are beginning once again to return to glory, to marvelous articulateness and vivid color, and nothing like it has been seen since the stained glass of Chartres. That is a good sign, but it requires that there be in our daily life a sense of freedom. I am not just talking about political freedom, I am talking about the freedom that comes when you know that you are it, forever and ever and ever, and it will be so nice when you die, because that will be a change, but it will come back some other way. When you know that, and you have seen through the whole mirage, then watch out, because there may be in you some seeds of hostility, some seeds of pride, some seeds of wanting to put down other people or wanting just to defy the normal arrangements of life. That is why in a Zen monastery, the novices are assigned the light duties and the more senior you get, the heavier your duties. The *roshi* is, for example, very often the one who cleans out the toilet. There is in this a kind of beautiful, almost princely aestheticism, because by reason of that order being observed all the time, the vast free energy that is contained in the system does not run amok. The understanding of Zen, the understanding of awakening, the understanding of mystical experience, is one of the most dangerous things in the world, and for a person who cannot contain it, it is like putting a million volts through your electric shaver. You blow your mind, and it stays blown.

One who goes off in that way is what is called a *pratyekabuddha*. This person is one who goes off into the transcendental world and is never seen again, and they have made a mistake from the standpoint of Buddhism, because in Buddhism there is no fundamental difference between the transcendental world and this everyday world. The *bodhisattva* does not go off into a *nirvana* and stay there forever and ever; they come back and live ordinary everyday life to help other beings to see through it, too. They do not come back because they feel they have some sort of solemn duty to help humankind and all that kind of pious cant. They come back because they see that the two worlds are the same, and they see all other beings as buddhas. To use a phrase of G. K. Chesterton, "But now a great thing in the street seems any human nod, where move in strange democracy, a million masks of God." It is fantastic to look at people and to see that they really, deep down inside, are enlightened, and they are it, they are faces of the divine. They look at you, and they say, "Oh no, but I'm not divine, I'm just ordinary little me." And you look at them in a funny way and you see the buddha nature, looking out of their eyes straight at you and saying, it is not, and saying it quite sincerely. That is why, when you get up against a great guru, the Zen master, they have a funny look in their eye. You say, "I have a problem, guru. I'm really mixed up and I don't understand." Then they look at you in this queer way, and you think "Oh dear me, they're reading my most secret thoughts. They are seeing all the awful things I am, all my cowardice, all my shortcomings." They are not doing anything of the kind. They are not even interested in such things. Instead they are looking at, if I may use Hindu terminology, the Shiva in you, and saying, "My God, Shiva, won't you come off it?"

The bodhisattva, as distinct from the *pratyeka-buddha*, does not go off into permanent withdrawn ecstasy, and they do not go into a kind of catatonic *samadhi*. That is all right and there are people who can do that because that is their vocation, their specialty. Just as a long thing is the long body of Buddha and a short thing is the short body of Buddha, if you really understand Zen, the Buddhist idea of enlightenment is not comprehended in the idea of the transcendental. It is neither comprehended in the idea of the ordinary, nor in terms of the infinite, nor in terms of the finite, nor in terms of the eternal, nor in terms of the temporal. These are all concepts.

I am not talking about the ordering of ordinary everyday life in a reasonable and methodical way and saying, "If you were nice people, that's what you would do." For heaven's sake, please do not be "nice people." Unless you do have that basic framework of a certain kind of order and a certain kind of discipline, however, the force of liberation will blow the world to pieces; it is too strong a current for the wire.

So then, it is terribly important to see beyond ecstasy. Ecstasy, yes, is the soft and lovely flesh, huggable and kissable, and that is very good. Yet beyond ecstasy are bones, what we call hard facts, the hard facts of everyday life. But we should not forget to mention the soft facts, and there are many of them. The hard fact, the world as seen in an ordinary everyday state of consciousness, however, is really no different from the world of supreme ecstasy. Let us suppose, as so often happens, that you think of ecstasy as insight, as seeing light. There is a Zen poem that says, "A sudden crash of thunder, the mind doors burst open and there sits the ordinary old man." There is this sudden vision, *satori*, and the doors of the mind

are blown apart and there sits the ordinary old man. Little
you. Lightning flashes, sparks shower. In one blink of your
eyes, you have missed seeing. Why? Because here is the light,
the light, every mystic in the world has seen the light, that
brilliant blazing energy brighter than a thousand suns that
is locked up in everything. Now, imagine this: Imagine you
are seeing it, like you see aureoles around buddhas, like you
see the beatific vision at the end of Dante's Paradiso. Vivid,
vivid, light so bright that it is like the clear light of the void in
the Tibetan *Book of the Dead,* beyond light it is so bright. You
watch it receding from you, and on the edges like a great star
that becomes a rim of red, and beyond that a rim of orange,
yellow, green, blue, indigo, violet, and you see this great *mandala* appearing, this great sun. Beyond the violet there is black,
like obsidian, not flat black, but transparent black, like lacquer
and again blazing out of the black as the yang comes from
the yin there comes sound. There is a sound so tremendous
with the white light that you cannot hear it, so piercing that
it seems to annihilate the ears. Then, along with the colors,
the sound goes down the scale in harmonic intervals, down,
down, down, until it gets to a deep thundering bass that is
so vibrant, that it turns into something solid, and you begin
to get the similar spectrum of textures. Now, all this time
you have been watching a kind of a thing radiating out, but
it says, You know, this isn't all I can do," and then rays start
going, going, dancing, and naturally the sound starts going,
waving, too, as it comes out. Then the textures start varying
themselves, and they say, "Well you have been looking at this

thing as I have been describing it so far in a flat dimension. Now let's add a third dimension, and it's going to come right at you now." Meanwhile, it says, "It's not that we're just going, going, like this, we're going to do little curlicues, we are going to go round and round like this." Then it says, "Well, that's just a beginning, we can go, here, there, and everywhere, making squares and turns, and then suddenly you see in all the little details that become so intense that all kinds of little subfigures are contained in what you thought were originally the main figures, and the sound starts going, amazing complexities of sound, all over the place, and this thing is going, going, going, and you think you are going to go out of your mind, and suddenly it turns into—why us, sitting around here. Thank you very much.

Notes

1. *Ku-tsun-hsu Yu-lu,* fascicle 1, chuan 4, pages 6, 7, and 24.

2. D.T. Suzuki, *Living by Zen* (Freeport, Maine: Samuel Weiser, 1972), 178.

3. It should be understood that Amitabha considered as "other" than oneself is not essentially different from what *jiriki* types of Buddhism call the innate Buddha-nature or original mind (*honshin*). This is easily understood from the analogy of the heartbeat. From one point of view, I (the conscious ego) am not making it happen, but from another point of view I (as something more or other than the ego) am doing it.

4. *Living by Zen,* 130.

5. *Living by Zen,* 179.